T0149451

A Sprinkle of Dust

A
Sprinkle
OF Dust

A MOTHER'S STRUGGLE WITH
LOSS AND HEALING

MARY SAAD ASSEL

iUniverse®

A SPRINKLE OF DUST
A MOTHER'S STRUGGLE WITH LOSS AND HEALING

iUniverse books may be ordered through booksellers or by contacting:

iUniverse
1663 Liberty Drive
Bloomington, IN 47403
www.iuniverse.com
1-800-Authors (1-800-288-4677)

ISBN: 978-1-5320-3221-9 (sc)
ISBN: 978-1-5320-3222-6 (e)

Print information available on the last page.

iUniverse rev. date: 09/11/2017

I don't believe you're dead. How can you be dead if I still feel you? Maybe like God, you changed into something different that I'll have to speak to in a different way, but you're not dead to me... and never will be. Sometimes when I get tired of talking to myself I talk to you.

—Alice Walker

You will lose someone you can't live without, and your heart will be badly broken, and the bad news is that you never completely get over the loss of your beloved. But this is also the good news. They live forever in your broken heart that doesn't seal back up. And you come through. It's like having a broken leg that never heals perfectly, but you learn to dance with the limp.

—Anne Lamott

Deep grief sometimes is almost like a specific location, a coordinate on a map of time. When you are standing in that forest of sorrow, you cannot imagine that you could ever find your way to a better place. But if someone can assure you that they themselves have stood in that same place, and now have moved on, sometimes this will bring hope.

—Elizabeth Gilbert

IN MEMORY OF MY SON MAZEN

Contents

Acknowledgements

I would like to acknowledge the support and commentaries of my writing group friends: Alex Morgan, Nancy Owen Nelson, and Joy Friedler. They helped me navigate through some of the most painful moments of my life while praising me along the way. My extended appreciation goes out to my editor Kate Robinson for revising and fine-tuning the manuscript. I would also like to thank my dear friends Ed and Martha Demerly for their editorial and moral support over the years, and Glenn O'Kray for his editorial comments and his wife Jane for her kind encouragement.

Many thanks to my family: my mother for her ongoing support; my sister Samerah and my siblings for filling in the blanks; my daughters and best friends, Rania and Dania, for their feedback and moral support; my resourceful son, Adam, for his quick-witted input; my precious daughter-in-law, Mona, for her heart-warming support; son-in-laws Emad and Karl; granddaughters Carina, Yasmine, Juliana, and Rhiana for believing in me; my grandsons Malik, Mahmoud, Ally, Jemail, and Mazen for cheering me on; and last but not least, my most gracious and precious husband, Ernie, for his outstanding support and editorial comments.

Prologue

Many authors inspired *A Sprinkle of Dust*, and perhaps my readers will also be familiar with these books: Eckhart Tolle's *Stillness Speaks*, Nahid Rachlin's *Persian Girls*, Brian Weiss's *Miracles Happen*, Mitch Albom's *The Timekeeper*, Gary Zukav's *Seat of the Soul*, and the spiritual writings of Gibran Khalil Gibran. One might also investigate the many fine classic works of literature that have emerged from many cultures in the Middle East from centuries past and into the present.

I lived in Africa and the Middle East for over twenty years, where I learned several languages and acquired several degrees while learning and writing about different cultures and traditions. It is my hope that my voice will help change the perception of Islam in America, that people will discover the commonalities between Eastern and Western faiths and cultures rather than focus upon the differences and shortcomings, as sparked by the dreadful day of 9/11/2001. Ultimately, all people just want to be happy and avoid suffering.

I was a wife at fifteen, a mother at sixteen, a widow at thirty-five, and heartbroken by the loss of my son at fifty. *A Sprinkle of Dust: A*

Mother's Struggle with Loss and Healing describes how I struggled to find hope and meaning in a challenging life despite facing the ultimate tragedy, the death of my firstborn child.

In the 1960s, my parents sent me from Michigan, the only home I'd ever known, to Africa to become a teenage bride and mother. After a period in war-torn Lebanon, I finally returned to the United States in the 1980s. My son, Mazen, grew up to be easygoing, self-confident, and dependable. He was blessed with an affectionate wife, three young children, and a positive outlook on life. He'd escaped death twice in Lebanon through the violent hands of militia groups only to be diagnosed with a terminal brain tumor when he was just thirty-one.

My first inclination was to research Mazen's tumor type to find ways to weave *hope* into his treatment. I typed the words "brain tumor" in my search engine and found hundreds of links to brain tumor publications and agencies. Within days, I received literature from the National and the American Brain Tumor societies. An astrocytoma is a tumor that arises from the star-shaped cells (astrocytes) that form the supportive tissue of the brain, and are also referred to as gliomas. The term elicited a fierce and cruel sensation. Gliomas sounded fatal. My heart stung. I wanted it to be still for a moment so that it could hear me curse the bitter tone of the word *fatal*.

The information on the page perplexed me, and I couldn't focus long enough to see what I was reading. My eye muscles were weakening, causing double vision. Under normal conditions, I could have read for hours and still feel energized. I didn't understand much, *maybe I didn't want to understand... I don't know...* but I read and re-read pages of facts and statistics regarding brain tumor patients and survival rates without much consolation. I didn't care about definitions and explanations. I was in search of a story—in search of *hope*. I feared the silence of eternity. I feared a dense, murky cloud would engulf me, robbing me of Mazen, my firstborn, the center of my life.

Mazen had a primary, grade III astrocytoma, a title assigned to one of the many tumors that infiltrate the brains of thousands of innocent people. I concluded that titles were just terms that people babble to label something new and unknown. Astrocytoma grade III does not always mean its carrier is going to die, and I didn't want to listen to doctors who told me so. Statements like "We're sorry, but there's nothing we can do. It's too late. Go home and write your will. You might only have two weeks to live," as the neurologist who worked at one of the highly trusted university hospitals in the state of Michigan had told Mazen, instilled anger and disbelief in me. What medical school trains doctors to play God or even to make such predictions? Do doctors think they can say what they want because the majority of their patients lack medical training and surrender their trust to them? What about *hope* and miracles? What about psychology and bedside manners?

I was desperate to do everything I could to help Mazen. After his doctors could do nothing more, I resorted to Christian healing. I drove across the deserts of Mexico to embrace the catholicon hands of a *curandera*, but she could not help either. Heartbroken, and torn between the crucifixion of my soul and submission to an unknown force of faith, I embarked on a spiritual journey that led me gradually to my sanctuary of peace and acceptance. My journey through the five stages of grief may serve as a guide to every parent in search of relief and understanding.

My journey through loss and grief has been both difficult and blessed. It is my hope that by revealing my pain and the months and years I spent groping through the darkness of my despair, that this act may ease the journey of other parents who have lost a child prematurely—at any age.

Coping with loss in any family can be painful and sometimes be one of the rockiest terrains to navigate in life. No matter how strong we think we are, we become weak and feel like our lives have been shaken to their foundations. Even though the majority of Muslims believe that death is an act of God and should not be questioned, the fact remains that the five stages of grief: denial, anger, bargaining, depression, and acceptance, are applicable to almost everyone regardless of cultural or religious backgrounds.

The first stage of grief, *denial*, felt as though the elements and properties of my body were staring me in the face, telling me that Mazen never really died. I wanted to believe that he went away for a short while and that there was nothing to grieve about. But when family and friends walked through my door to comfort me or drop off a meal, the hardness of my limbs and heart anchored me in my seat and forced me to display a smile. I knew from the dreadful sound of my soul that my harp and lyre had been broken—and that *time* was not going to bridge the gulf between Mazen and me. All I had left was the scent of his clothing. I had always walked through life thinking that my heart was made of steel, but I was wrong. The blood pushing against my artery walls alerted me that my heart was overworked and fragile. It felt like a pitcher overflowing with tears of lead, causing my chest to swell and my back to bend. I told my heart to hold still. I was trying to deny reality; a reality that was persecuting the faint hope I had left to inform me that Mazen was never coming back. I'd go to bed each night crying and praying that God would enlighten me of the mystery that lies behind life and death, but never found rest. The rising of each morning sun was no longer perceived as a new day, but rather, as additional confirmation that Mazen had wandered off beyond my reach. I sensed that life would never be the same again and that my spirit would forever be crushed. The more I thought about my loss, the more the odor of mortality hung in the air.

> Denial is the first of the five stages of grief. It helps us to survive the loss. In this stage, the world becomes meaningless and overwhelming. Life makes no sense. We are in a state of shock and denial. We go numb.
>
> —David Kessler and Elizabeth Kubler Ross
> *On Grief and Grieving*, 2005

In the first five chapters, I share my memories of Mazen, my fear of losing him, and the details of his illness. Chapters 6 through 13 are aligned with denial, the first stage of grief, as I struggled with accepting his death. As life unfolded, my anxiety and grief transformed into anger and aversion (Chapters 14-15). I resented living and being left behind. As I progressed along the path to acceptance, I imagined I would have a chance to bargain with God (Chapter 16), but lost and adrift, I fell into a depression (Chapters 17-18). Eventually I reached a state of equanimity and acceptance—the final stage of grief (Chapter 19). *A Sprinkle of Dust* is ultimately my personal story of grief, surrender, and reconciliation—how I navigated the rocky shores of loss to rediscover joy.

—Mary Saad Assel, PhD
October 2017

There were many ways of breaking a heart. Stories were full of hearts broken by love, but what really broke a heart was taking away its dream—whatever that dream might be.

—Pearl S. Buck

Chapter 1

Melancholy and Decay

The messenger of death had spread its wings around Mazen, giving me very little time to reflect on the miracles that might yet save him. Sighing in my agony, I sat diagonally from the heavily timbered oak coffee table in his living room and stared occasionally at my thirty-three-year-old son resting on his recliner.

I had followed God's teachings faithfully with hope that He would somehow intervene. I questioned Him at each waking moment and begged Him to lift my spirits and make things better. He didn't. Buried in thought and the pressure of faith in its iron framework, I uttered, and then typed across the screen of my laptop, words that flowed from the dark labyrinth of my mind.

At the beginning of Mazen's illness, my writing routine had become so habitual and involuntary that he asked me with a touch of melancholy and decay in his voice, "Mom, you do a lot of writing. Are you writing a book? Am I in it?"

"Yes, oh yes . . . you're in my book, Mazen. You're certainly an integral part of it."

Not to add fuel to the fiery tortures of his heart, I refrained from telling him that not only was he part of it, but he was the guiding light of my manuscript.

On Thursday morning, April 12, 2001, Mazen's nurse said, "Mary, I am so sorry, but Mazen's body is shutting down and we're reaching the end. It started last week, one organ at a time, and now, his lungs and heart are failing."

The last ray of light vanished behind the darkness of my wondering soul. *What does she mean? Have I been living a fantasy for recreation's sake?* I wanted her to tell me that by some miraculous and divine intervention, *Mazen is going to live, not... he's reaching the end.*

I studied her compassionate face. "You've been sensitive and supportive during the past few months. Please don't say, *'this is the end.'* You taught me how to care for Mazen and now, everything is over? You're telling me I will no longer see his tender face?"

Where will he go? Will he drift away to some moss-grown world beyond, a world that no one has returned from to describe?

I wanted to scream, but I held back.

Mazen's nurse had become a family friend. She taught us nursing skills so we could look after Mazen while she was away. She embraced our Arab-Muslim culture and spoke in an attenuated voice about the culture of the dying. I couldn't blame her for recording Mazen's vital signs, but to hear the truth was painful, and I preferred that she didn't verbalize it. She had trained me enough to know things weren't looking good, but *hope* was all I had and I wanted to stop hope from moldering away.

When I'd read Mazen's medical report on the day he was diagnosed, it did not give me any indication of *hope*. Nevertheless, I insisted on defying the medical community by giving vigor to this profound term. I allowed myself to assign a new meaning to it, despite knowing that I might be deceived as I was when Mahmoud, Mazen's father, had died fifteen years earlier. From birth, Mazen was the heavenly light that illuminated his father's face and if the dead could weep, Mahmoud would have flooded the world with his tears over what was happening to Mazen. When Mahmoud was ill, I'd equated the word *hope* with *recovery* though he never recovered. I believed that even *fraudulent hope* with its nasty taste was more jubilant than confronting the reality of his fate. Mahmoud, now Mazen.

If they think that people with a terminal illness need to know their fate so that they can prepare themselves for death, then how do we interpret what a lady once wrote to Bernie Siegel, a doctor who resigned from treating his patients medically and transformed his practice to helping the terminally ill find comfort in *hope.* I quote from his book *How To Live Between Office Visits:*

> I was told many times that I had not long to live, and I was very ill. . . So I made out a will, gave away my valued treasures to family and friends, I bought a dog, took more vitamins, started exercising and eating better, laughed more and put in the backyard wildlife habitat, my life's desire. If I was going to die, I might as well die doing all the things I wanted to do.

It's never too late. I hoped that God, who had become my mountain peak of faith some years prior to Mazen's diagnosis, might still intervene. I adopted the habit of drawing in a long, deep, and tremulous breath each time I thought about the possibility of Mazen overcoming the powerful invasive disease. Why say "*it's over*" when doctors, science, and medical reports can be challenged? The answer was not too far off to seek. I steeled myself to oppose the status quo and to believe that there was hope.

When doctors diagnosed my husband, Mahmoud, with lung cancer just fifteen years prior, estimating he had one year to live, the world became gloomy and despondency brooded in my heart as his condition deteriorated by the day. My fear of losing him compelled me to challenge science and even though I failed repeatedly in my use of clinical trials and alternative medicine, I wasn't closing any doors with Mazen.

Although I had placed my memories of Mahmoud to rest and remarried seven years later, those aching moments of my life still haunt me. At the time, I was like a stunned bird that had to reteach itself to fly. It took years of rising and falling, but I learned to refocus and maintain my physical and mental equilibrium; that is, until my son was diagnosed with terminal cancer. With Mazen, I don't know how much of my *hope* was a projection or the synergy of positive forces beyond my control, but I chose to deal with cancer anew and pray that he, like many other miraculous survivors, was going to defeat it.

Chapter 2

Kidnapped

It was a hot and muggy summer afternoon when my flight landed in Dakar, Senegal in 1966. The moment I reached the landing and began to take my first step down the aircraft stairs, the heat battered my face as though I had stuck it in an oven. I clutched my husband's hand and wondered about the rest of my life.

Is this Africa? Is this my new home? Tears of flame traveled down my cheeks. I felt as if I resided outside my body. I feared I wasn't going to survive, even a day. The change from the United States to Senegal was like moving from the elements of light to those of blindness. It wasn't until I walked inside the air-conditioned building and saw the beautiful faces of my cousins and my Aunt Khadija did I feel the continents connecting through blood.

I leaned against a pillar for a brief moment, caught in a moment of wonder and revelation. I swayed to and fro. I silently bathed in my aunt's brown, mulberry shaped eyes. I kissed the air and chanted in my heart . . .I love my mother's sister. She was plump. Her eyes focused directly at me and seemed paralyzed and motionless. Her lips were set like straight lines that called for a miracle to make them shift. Armed by her stern but loving presence, I felt peace and serenity. I tried to find my mother's twin as my aunt stretched her arms to greet me, but instead, the aroma of my deceased grandmother filled the air. I smiled. She smiled back. I missed my mother and my aunt sensed my pain. She assured me that I would be fine and that she would crown me with her love. And she did. Her love was profound and special, manifested in the form of infinite compassion. Aunt Khadija was the absentee mother I was yearning for.

The streets were filled with the bustling of people and cars. Huts were dispersed in lots between the high rises, and the boutiques were loaded with traditional Senegalese garments and fabrics. My focus vanished as soon as my husband, who was sitting in the front passenger seat, turned his head around. "That store on the corner is mine. I am going to turn you into a salesperson. You're going to help me with the business, right?" He chuckled and placed his hand on the driver's shoulder. I didn't know what to make of his remark or whether I should even smile back. I grew weary as I became transfixed with a monstrous baobab tree that governed the corners of Marche Sandaga, the main market of Dakar.

Dakar and all surrounding cities were beautiful and rather than rob me of the treasures of my country, the new environment gave me new insights. I learned new languages. I learned how to become a wife and a mother. Most of all, I learned to glorify myself with my children, the roses of my earth.

Ten years later, I was again preparing for a new transition, a new home, a new life.

Mazen, almost ten years old, was healthy and easygoing, and smiled each time I gazed at him. "I love you, Mama," he said each day before he left the house, or each night when he went to bed. The only time I'd taken him to the doctor after he had turned five was for annual check-ups and vaccination updates. I had no idea that, within the weeks and months to come, I would experience the abject fear of losing him not once, not twice, but three times.

I taught him how to play Scrabble and Monopoly, and he taught me how to play chess. We challenged each other by claiming that the loser would have to do whatever the winner wanted for the rest of the evening. He'd usually win, and I'd find myself baking his favorite cakes or cheating by asking my expert sandwich maker, Dania, to help me stack a pile of sandwiches on a fancy platter.

"Does his majesty need anything else?" I'd facetiously inquire.

"No, thank you. This is enough," he would say, a gleam in his eyes.

During this sweet era, my husband and I decided to leave Dakar, Senegal and move to Lebanon. I felt anxiety similar to my state of mind when I'd first arrived in Senegal in 1966. When I broke the news to Mazen on June 5, 1977, he was sitting on the edge of his bed playing his guitar and singing. His lithe fingers moved gracefully across the strings and his lips blossomed like rosebuds, emitting words with a lyrical fragrance that sweetened the room. To avoid breaking the rhythm, I sat next to him and touched his shoulder. He played the tune of *Attend Moi*, a song by a French artist whose name I can't recall.

The blue lyrics carried my spirit to a higher plateau, like a butterfly in a summer breeze. Articulate beyond his years, Mazen often touched people with his speech, even when he was quite small. As soon as he paused, I gathered up my courage to speak. "Mazen, you are definitely talented. I don't mean to interrupt, but I have something to say. Your father and I have decided to move to Lebanon."

"What? Why?" He raised his eyebrows and propped his guitar behind him.

I didn't know what to tell him. I thought we must be insane to relocate to a country where, for over ten years, a civil war had draped its skies with the dust of firearms and bombs. According to media reports, missiles and bullets were flying back and forth between the western and eastern rooftops of Beirut, a city that had divided in the early '70s into two semi-governing regimes with drastic political and religious differences.

The once glistening city was shattered with the rumbling thunder of explosions, and its people, young and old, helplessly waited for something good or bad to come their way. Innocent people were dying and peace talks were failing. Determined to seek revenge for the death of their loved ones, many angered young men committed acts of vengeance, that along with poorly trained militias, made matters worse by increasing the unpredictability of violent acts. The Syrian army was gradually spreading its semi-totalitarian regime across the country under the pretext of military aid for peace.

"But I want to stay in Senegal with my friends."

"Listen, we can make this fun. We'll go to Paris, buy a new car, and drive from there to Lebanon. This will give you a chance to see new people, new countries, and learn more about the world. What do you say?"

"What can I say? I don't think I have a choice. When are we going?"

"Well, you'll be out of school in a couple of weeks so, maybe then…? Why don't you break the news to your sisters and tell them that we'll be leaving during the first week of July?"

"Why me? Why don't you tell them?"

"Oh, it might be more exciting for them to hear it from you first."

I called Mahmoud, who had left for Lebanon a month earlier to purchase a condominium and to register the children in a reliable French school, to tell him what I'd suggested to Mazen. He chuckled and said, "That's a great idea. I'll meet you in Paris on July 1."

Excited about the trip from Paris to Lebanon, I called my mother, who was living in Michigan, and asked her if she'd like to join us. She agreed to meet me in Paris around July 10.

I flew into Paris from Senegal on July 1 to purchase furniture and to prepare for the trip to Lebanon.

I left Mazen, Rania, and Dania with my friend Wafaa in Senegal while I went to meet Mahmoud. A week later, I asked Wafaa to send the children to Paris. I greeted them at Charles De Gaulle Airport with hugs and kisses, but at the hotel, Mazen said, "Mama, I don't feel good." He looked weak and pale, and his forehead felt warm to my touch. I called the hotel receptionist to ask for directions to the closest clinic or hospital.

Within a matter of minutes, Mazen became feeble and walked with extraordinary caution from fear that he might fall. His dark black irises turned sickly against the yellowish sclera of his eyes. He needed immediate medical attention, and I couldn't wait for his father, who was out shopping for a car. The receptionist, whom I had befriended after staying at this same hotel each time I went to Paris, agreed to watch Rania and Dania, who were six and eight at the time, until my return. Five feet tall, Mazen weighed about one hundred and fifteen pounds, too heavy for me to carry. I wrapped my arm around his shoulders, leaned him against my torso, directed my daughters to trail behind us, and rushed to the elevator.

I promised Rania and Dania that I'd be back soon and when we arrived in the hotel lobby, I explained to the receptionist that we were going to the nearest hospital. She promised to take good care of the girls.

We exited to the street and I waved down a cab. I helped Mazen climb into the cab and directed the driver to take me to the hospital. By the time we'd arrived, Mazen had fallen asleep on my lap.

"Let's go, Mazen! We're here."

"I can't walk. Please carry me…"

I carried him with extreme difficulty into the emergency room, took one look at the front desk receptionist, and broke down in tears. "Please help me. My son is very ill."

She rushed me to a back room where I lay him on a stretcher. A doctor examined him and said, "I don't know what's wrong with him. I'm sorry, but there's nothing I can do."

I thought it strange he couldn't tell me what was wrong and would send me away. Alarmed, I asked for a list of hospitals in the area and traveled from hospital to hospital wondering if Mazen had caught some deadly virus when I'd left him with my friend Wafaa for a week. I remained overwhelmed until I reached the American hosptial where a medical team greeted me at the door. They rolled him away on a stretcher and insisted I remain in the waiting room. I called the hotel and the receptionist gave the receiver to my husband, desperately waiting to hear from me. "Tell me where you are so I can meet you there," Mahmoud said, alarm seeping into his voice.

Someone ordered an immediate blood and urine test and within thirty minutes, a tall, muscular, female physician tapped my shoulder and said, "Your son is going to be just fine. The urine test showed that he has *hepatite viral* which can be treated with rest and diet." I didn't care to ask what *hepatite viral* meant as long as I knew *he is going to be just fine.*

Mahmoud rushed into the hospital emergency cubicle with tears streaming down his cheeks. The doctor looked at him and said, "Monsieur, your son is going to be fine. You can take him home now."

I explained to her that we were visitors and that we were staying in a hotel and planned to travel to Lebanon by car. She insisted that we restrict Mazen's diet and give him at least five days of rest prior to traveling.

Mazen became stronger each day. By the fifth day, my mother had arrived from Michigan, and we prepared for our trip to Lebanon. Excited, I traced out the countries we would be traveling through on a map and figured it might take us about ten days to arrive in Lebanon. Mahmoud drove most of the time. He told jokes and spooky stories about the people of his village, and stopped to make hotel reservations in the evenings. We crossed through the cities of Geneva, Milan, Venice, Budapest, Bucharest, Sofia, Istanbul, Ankara, Latakia, and finally, Tripoli, located in northern Lebanon. We stopped for a few hours, or sometimes an entire afternoon, to admire the landscape and visit the cultural and religious monuments as well as appease our hunger with a variety of exotic foods at local restaurants.

Exhausted but happy that we'd finally arrived in Lebanon, we didn't realize the Syrian army was stationed in almost every section of Tripoli, one of the largest cities in northern Lebanon. Within ten minutes of entering Tripoli, the Syrian army fired warning shots around our car. We froze as my mother began to scream. "I told you you're making a mistake! Lebanon is not safe. You should have relocated to America, not Lebanon."

Mahmoud snapped back. "I don't care for the United States! I made a mistake by not paying close attention to the Syrian checkpoint!"

Mother-in-law jokes had become a reality. She shriveled up and he remained silent.

Mahmoud stopped the car. The militiaman walked as though drilling holes in the ground with his feet, staring at each of one of us. He sternly cautioned Mahmoud for not stopping when he first saw the checkpoints. Mahmoud explained that he wasn't used to checkpoints and promised he would be much more careful in the future.

From then on, we paid close attention to our surroundings and hoped we would reach our new home in west Beirut safely. Rania and Dania wept, and Mazen held my hand tightly repeating, "I wish we hadn't come here. *Tata* is right. We should have gone to Michigan."

Living in Beirut was a troubling adjustment. I didn't know who was who. Soldiers and militia groups surrounded our neighborhood. It didn't take my children long, though, to make friends and within weeks, it was hard to keep them at home. They played ping-pong and soccer with the neighbors and they eventually spoke more Arabic than French or English. I didn't bother them as long as they obeyed our directive to be home by 6:00 p.m. They made more friends than I wanted them to and they declared that they enjoyed living in Lebanon more than they had in Senegal. Happy with their adjustment, I had no idea that soon, what felt like a warm and pleasant evening, would turn into a string of terrifying tribulations.

One evening during the following summer, a year after my difficult adjustment to life in war-torn Lebanon, Mazen was nowhere to be found. We lived on the fourth floor of a condominium complex, and after standing on the balcony and yelling Mazen's name for over ten minutes, I became desperate. I ran downstairs and began knocking on doors. I hoped to find him visiting with neighbors. I asked his friend Salim, who stood quietly near the curb in front of the parking lot, if he had seen Mazen. Casually, he said, "Oh, he went with some guys in a car about a half hour ago. I thought maybe he knew them."

I panicked and ran back upstairs to call his father, Mahmoud, who had opened a business less than a block away from home. He came running, frightened and alarmed, which worried me even more. He immediately called his older brother Ibrahim, his friends, relatives, and neighbors, and asked them to join us in our search. After about two hours of deliberating with them, Mahmoud concluded that Mazen had been kidnapped. He contacted the Lebanese internal security forces, two senators, and three friends from the Ministry of Justice. He invited them to our home with hope that they might contact and pressure local militia heads to help us find Mazen's kidnappers. He paced back and forth in our living room, threatening reprisal to whomever had taken Mazen.

By midnight, I feared I would never again see my only son. I ran toward Mahmoud, pushed him against the wall, and screamed, "I want my son! Bring me back my son!"

I had heard stories about children being kidnapped, and the only thing racing through my mind was the thought that he was being abused physically and mentally. I had left Senegal, a country that had become my own, to live in Lebanon, a nation that had morphed into the beast that gazed down at me and opened its mouth, quivering and thirsty for blood. I screamed as I was calling my Lord, begging him to send my son back to me. My reflections of Mazen's sparkly eyes and dimples were unreachable. I embraced the shadows of the weeping gloom around me, overtaken by the power of a soldier prepared for battle. I was determined to find my son. I felt like a cannonball ready to explode.

I turned to the men, who were still filling the air with heavy smoke from their cigarettes and cigars. "If you can't find him, I will," I exclaimed, and ran out of the house. The full moon at midnight gazed down at me as though to say, *I will help you*. Releasing my fears, I ran down the block with the hope that Mazen's kidnappers would miraculously return him. I thought I was dreaming when I ran into Salim, who stood alongside his older brother. In a petrified voice, he yelled, "We found him!"

"Where is he?" I cried back.

"He's hiding in a dark corner behind a brick wall. I couldn't get him to come with me. Follow me. I will show you," he said, his voice and face darkening in sadness.

Mazen was sitting on the ground with his face hidden between his hands, weeping. Frightened, he jumped when he heard me call his name. "Mama, I'm scared. What if they come back?"

"They will never come back! Your father and uncle made sure that they would be prosecuted to the letter of the law! Let's go home and talk. I will never let you leave my sight again!

I rushed him home.

"Now that you're under your covers and warm, please talk to me. Your sisters are making you some tea." I said softly.

A waterfall of words began to tumble from Mazen. Mahmoud, who was standing at the door, ready to listen to everything, secretly put his fingers on his lips as a gesture for me not to interrupt.

"Well, I was running around the corner to grab the soccer ball and all of the sudden, several men jumped out of their jeep, grabbed me, and threw me in the back seat. At first, I wanted to yell, but it was as though I lost my voice. Then, when I was finally able to capture my words, I shouted, "Take me home!" A man with bloodshot eyes sitting next to me told me to shut up. He taped my mouth and blindfolded me. They drove around in circles and stopped in an area where I could hear the voices of women chatting and children playing. But the voices got softer and softer and faded into the distance. I was scared. Then, one of the men yanked my arm, lugged me out of the jeep and dragged me across the ground. Seconds later, he made me stand up. He took me by the neck, opened a door and threw me down the stairs. I was crying and choking at the same time. I couldn't breathe. I was shocked when they started laughing and chuckling. I wondered how they could do this to me and laugh about it. I could barely breathe. I was afraid they would kill me. I didn't want to die. Then, maybe ten minutes later, I realized that my hands were free. I found the guts to take the tape off my mouth. They didn't react. I didn't want to take the blindfold off because I didn't want to see their faces again. Then, the room went silent. My limbs froze. I was scared to stand up, but I took the blindfold off and looked around me. There were no windows.

I was in a dungeon. The walls were strong and weren't even painted, and there was a chair in the middle of the room with chains tied to its sides. I saw these kinds of things in the movies, but I couldn't believe that I was actually sitting in a torture chamber. Everything was spooky. I wanted to cover my eyes so that I wouldn't see anything, but my hands were trembling. I wrung them hoping that I could stop the trembling, but my whole body started shaking. I knew then that you would never find me. I cried myself to sleep. I don't know how much time had passed, when I heard the door open.

"'Get up,' they shouted. "We're taking you back! Your father is more influential than we thought, and it doesn't seem we're going to make any money off you, at least not for the moment.'"

I wrapped my arms around him and tried not to let him feel my despair at hearing his heart-rending story. It was 5 a.m. I prayed the sun would lift into the morning sky.

After years of living in a war-torn country and surviving the rumblings of bombshells and bullets, I learned that survival isn't always an option. We could hide from bombs, we could survive kidnapping, but we couldn't hide from the messenger of death.

Chapter 3

I Love You

Lebanon had become my new home despite the tragic war that lasted for over a decade. There is no such thing as freedom from or reasoning with war. On days when there was heavy shelling, everyone would gather in the stairwell. Surrounded by brick walls, it seemed safe. Yet, we all knew that no one was safe. While opposing militia groups were imprisoned between the chiseling winds of deadly attacks, my neighbors were whispering to each other stories of shame and disgust. I refused to join them. I took my chances and stayed in my condominium. If I wasn't studying for my exams, I played loud music to drown the sound of missiles and shed the fear of losing a loved one. I took my chances as I drove the streets and hustled through the marketplace. I fumbled through fruits and vegetables and breathed the polluted air, searching for a sense of normality in a country where nothing seemed normal. I tried hard to suppress my fears, but when overburdened with panic, I would look upon the merchant's face and smile. I'd listen to my heart and hear God's voice assuring me that I was going to make it back home despite the foolishness of my actions, actions that were beyond my own cognizance and understanding.

In June of 1985, Rania, Dania, and I left Lebanon to spend the summer with my parents in Detroit. Mazen, eighteen at the time, stayed with his father to prepare for a retake of the Baccalaureate Part II national exam that would take place in mid-July. Demographic tensions stemming from twisted political and religious affiliations that had originally led to civil war, intensified between East and West Beirut a month after I had left.

Our condominium complex was struck by several bombs. Mazen, standing on the porch at the time of the explosions, had leaned sideways to evade shrapnel shells. He crawled back into the house only to find that the TV set had shattered and his cat, covered with white powdery residue, was hiding underneath the brown velvet chair in the family room. War was no longer simply occurring around our home—our home and our neighbors had become war casualties.

From across the ocean, the breaking news struck me like lightning. Several of my neighbors and their children had been killed. Over the phone, Mahmoud sounded terrified, but reassured me that they were fine. Mazen, frightened and immobilized, sounded downhearted and panicky.

He broke into tears. "I love you, Mama."

"I love you too, sweetheart," I said, discouraged and frantically wondering how I would get him out of Lebanon.

The next day, I rented a home and sent for Mazen. I decided not to return to Lebanon, at least not until the civil war had settled. Mahmoud, a Lebanese patriot, clung to all that he possessed—his assets and emotional ties—and refused to join us. Unfortunately, in December of the same year, he was diagnosed with terminal lung cancer and given just a year to live. We returned to Lebanon in January of 1986.

The thought of losing Mahmoud set me off in different directions. I'd fancied having a husband to share life with until we became crippled by old age, especially so because we were both young. Death was almost always a word reserved for the elderly and the mere thought of Mahmoud dying forced me into a state of dysphoria. I tried to put on a strong front, but quite often, I couldn't talk to the children without feeling as if a fishbone had lodged in my throat. While polishing mirrors and furniture, I drowned in my tears on the days we were not at the doctor's office or in the hospital running a dose of chemotherapy. And on the days that my eyes were swollen by too much weeping, I'd instruct the maid not to answer the doorbell. I couldn't talk to anyone without feeling weighed down and helpless.

I fought Mahmoud's disease with mental and physical ferocity from the beginning. But toward the end, prayers and candlelight vigils were my means of comfort as the echoes of his constant coughing traveled through the joint walls of our condominium to the ears of our neighbors, who in kind words would say, in effect, that they were praying for his relief.

I wasn't sure what sort of relief they referred to, but perhaps the change of his skin from a normal pinkish tone to a duller, darker, grayish hue was a death signal to all those who saw him. He was approaching the end.

The intensity of my affection increased with the intensity of my war against cancer. I was hoping to turn the vigor of my love into a powerful, invasive treatment that might triumph over the malignant cells residing within him, but I failed. I was perplexed by my un-precipitated, poignant affection for Mahmoud. I was beginning to wonder . . . *is this love*?

I blamed my arranged marriage for my inability to connect with Mahmoud on a heart-throbbing level. I could never say the words *"I love you"* to him. I had learned to care for him over the years, but I never associated *care* with *love*. I believed that love between couples was nothing more than a four-letter word and that "star-crossed lovers" was a term coined by Shakespeare to captivate his audience and give the relationship between Romeo and Juliet more credence. When Mahmoud gave me gifts, he lightheartedly followed his gesture with, "Aren't you going to say *I love you?*" but I always replied with a smile. His illness brought me to the realization that I was wrong and that *true love* was something that is not only real, but can be felt willingly and joyfully. My love for Mahmoud had finally exposed itself. It shook the ground beneath me like an earthquake.

I held him in my arms night after night throughout his illness and whispered, "I love you..." over and over again. I no longer sealed love, with trepidation, between my lips. My words took flight with sensual fervor like "the winged seraphs of heaven" that connected Edgar Allen Poe with his beloved Annabel Lee.

Mahmoud confided in me one night. "Even though I am very ill, if this is what it takes for me to hear you say *I love you* after twenty years of marriage, then wherever this illness is leading me, I'm willing to go."

With tears like burning flames running down my cheeks, I realized that not only does love harmonize one's being, but it can also be painful.

Mahmoud died on December 10, 1986. At home, on the evening of his death, relatives, neighbors, and friends stopped by to pay their respects. Oblivious to my surroundings, I held onto one of Mahmoud's shirts and cried for hours. The faint odor of his shirt wrestled its way into my nostrils and gave me an escalating high. I hoped to draw a bond between the living and the dead, but instead, my pain grew deeper. Mazen, who had left his uncle's house where the men were paying their respects, came home, walked into the living room where I was sitting, took me to bed, and held my hand until I fell asleep.

The next morning, we drove to Chacra, Mahmoud's hometown, situated thirty miles from Beirut and a few miles west of the Israeli border. Mahmoud's parents were deceased, but their home, which appeared neglected and abandoned, was used to prepare the corpse for the evening prayer. Mahmoud's two brothers and a sister, who lived in Africa, asked that we delay the burial until their arrival the following day.

Islam encourages readers of Quranic verses to surround the dead until burial. The verses may be read by family members or by hired individuals. I had engaged two young men to spend the night and read the Quran over Mahmoud, but the sound of rocket shells echoed through the valleys and caused everyone to fall into a state of panic.

There was a lot tension that year between Israelis and Palestinians. The Israelis launched an air attack that evening and from fear of a ground attack, hundreds of young men, regardless of their involvement in the Palestinian-Israeli conflict, fled the village by midnight, Mazen included. I spent the night alone, praying over Mahmoud's corpse. By 9:00 a.m., Mazen returned. Mahmoud's two brothers and sister also arrived from Africa. The funeral began.

Over twenty men approached the front door that led to the living room where I stood. I held my arms across the door like a child guarding her jewels. I had hoped to prolong the moment. They asked me to move aside and not to join the procession. I trailed behind the procession anyway, taking slow, but heavy steps as I stomped my anger into the ground and cursed at the furnace of my pain. My sisters-in-law were in the front yard of their parents' home, along with several other women, performing a wailing ritual. They wept and beat their faces with the dust of the earth and initiated conversations with the dead. They conversed with their parents and with Mahmoud about sweet memories and moments of bliss. They walked in circles, shouting, "Allahu Akbar... La Illaha Illa Allah... Allahu Akbar... La Illaha Illa Allah"—"God is great...There is no God, but God"... raising their handkerchiefs to and fro.

Then, suddenly, one of the women approached me. She said in a firm tone, "Where are you going? Stay here with us. Women are forbidden to join in the burial process."

Baffled that she agreed with traditional mores and the status quo, I ignored her comment and continued my route. The men were too far ahead to notice I was following them.

I had lost my husband. My children had lost their father. I didn't think anyone had the right to force me to follow tradition. Rania and Dania were holding on to me with more strength than I ever thought they had. The sky seemed to be caving in when a blue lightning bolt landed heavily on my shoulder and a strange voice that rang in my ears ordered me to let go of Mahmoud. Petrified and numbed by the experience, I froze for a moment, wondering if my body had separated from my mind. I began to walk at a reduced speed to gather my senses. Coming to terms with death was something I needed to work on, and it certainly wouldn't happen on my way to the cemetery.

I wasn't able to focus on what transpired at the time, but as I think about it today, setting aside the philosophy of mind-body problems or physicalism, I credit that God communicates with us in unconventional ways. I believe at that moment, He sent His Angels to warn me to draw back and to let Mahmoud's soul unite with the cosmic energy of the dead. Perhaps the warning was an act of kindness. God solidified my tears and gave me a moment of temporary relief and deliverance. As I approached the procession, I ignored the despicable stares of the men whose eyes banned me from joining them.

Occasionally, along the one-mile walk, I glimpsed Mazen's dark hair, a stark contrast with the graying heads of the older men. The corpse was ritually wrapped in a white *kafan* and covered with a bright green cloth, with Quranic verses written in gold thread around the edges. Islam encourages there be no barriers between the corpse and the Earth, and a coffin would have prevented this. Every now and then, Mazen would shift under the weight of his father's corpse. He shifted his burden from the outer to the inner end of his shoulder, causing the stretcher to swerve from side to side and to drift back over the shoulders of the townspeople who had opted to share in transporting Mahmoud to his final resting place. They took turns to relieve each other, but not Mazen. Whether they participated in the ritual out of affection for Mahmoud or by divine invocation, they hauled him away like robots extirpated of human emotion. They did not look toward Mazen or even say a word to him. Perhaps they thought it was his duty to endure the physical and emotional pain resulting from his father's death and to recalibrate his position in life by forfeiting his youth and assuming a level of maturity tenfold.

After arriving at the cemetery, the men circled the area around Mahmoud's grave with an Imam standing close by. Then a young boy came running toward me. He stopped abruptly. "They told me to tell you they would literally carry you away if you didn't keep your distance."

"Tell them I will. I promise…"

I watched from a distance. Mazen seemed as if programmed to follow rituals and do as he was told. He laid the stretcher on the ground, removed the green cover and with the assistance of a few men, lowered his father's body into the hollow grave. Nothing was said. Custom was complete. The scene gave me confirmation that men were emotionally more controlled than women, and to be in their company redefined my femininity, at least for the moment.

I turned my head away, and wiped away my tears while tripping over the cobblestones beneath my feet, trying to find my way out of the cemetery. Staring at empty verandas and the cloudy sky, I noticed an old man leaning on a cane, walking in my direction. He stopped for a moment, shook his head repeatedly, and cleared his throat. "And you thought that your loved ones will live forever…"

I stiffened for a moment to connect the dots meandering between us until I realized he'd just taught me a lesson—*never take your loved ones for granted.* But then, I wasn't sure that such a lesson could have prepared me for Mahmoud's death.

Chapter 4

The Lasting Aroma of Death

Mahmoud's death threw me into a state of despair. I didn't want to get up in the morning and face the world. Life became meaningless and my desire to return to the routine of daily living lessened by the day. I slept more and ate less. I told Salam, the housekeeper, to take charge of the kitchen and to bring my meal to the bedroom. I stared at food as if staring at an enemy. After a few bites and struggling with my fork, I'd set my dish on the nightstand and ask Salam to make coffee.

She would gaze at me, then try to make light of the situation. "Am I not a good cook? Please eat a few more bites and prove to me that you like my cooking."

"No, Salam. I'm just not hungry. Thank you."

Mazen, who had taken over the business, ran it ten hours a day, six days a week. He was facing some investment challenges and within a few weeks, he came to my bedside. "Mama, please get up. Here, I can massage your weak leg and bring feeling back to it. Please go take a shower so we can go to work together."

I tried, but my leg was too numb. I was experiencing what my neurologists had referred to as post-polio syndrome or a cluster of potentially disabling signs and symptoms that appear decades after the initial polio illness. My symptoms were progressive, causing joint weakness in the left leg. For days, I'd try to walk, lose my balance and fall. I made it a point to stay home, thinking Mazen didn't need me at his dad's business.

"Mazen, I'm sorry, but I can't today. I will try harder tomorrow."

I spent the evening massaging and exercising my leg with hope that I could work up blood flow in my leg and build the courage I needed to rejoin the outside world. By the time I went to bed, I was exhausted mentally and physically.

I woke up the next morning startled by the sonorous ring of the phone, not realizing that it was already past 9:00 a.m.

"Hello."

"Hi, Mama, I need to talk to you about something."

"Sure. I'll take a quick shower and meet you at the business in twenty minutes. I don't feel any numbness in my leg. Thanks for letting me sleep in," I joked.

"No, you don't have to come. I can talk to you over the phone."

"All right, what's up?"

I could hear him puffing a cigarette as he took a deep breath and said, "I want to go back to school. We need to sell this business and return to the United States. We don't have family here anymore and I want to finish my degree. I want to major in engineering design technology, maybe biomedical engineering, I'm not sure."

"Okay . . . Okay. Can I think about this for a second?" I said, wondering what to say next.

"I have thirty-three credit hours and I feel like I'm wasting my time here. Even though I loved my father, this is not what I want to do for the rest of my life," he replied with a sliver of self-pity in his voice.

"Of course," I said, weakened and saddened by the loss of my husband and the thought that Mazen was going to leave me too. I tried to keep my selfishness to myself.

"I agree and I want you to go back to school, but it may take at least six months to liquidate everything and sell the property. I can't do it alone. Together, we might be able to make it happen sooner," I said after probing for a reasonable response.

"All right, I'll meet you halfway. I'll stay until May. That will give me a chance to sign up for summer classes," he said with determination.

"Good. I'll be there in a bit so we can talk more."

Then, I heard him yell, "Hey, hey, what are you doing? You can't just take that and walk away without paying. Who are you?" He dropped the phone and all I could hear was static.

Oh my God! Something is wrong!

I dressed as fast as I could, darted out the door, and scurried down the stairs, skipping every other step and wondering what happened to the numbness in my leg. As I ran out the glass doors of the building, a neighbor, returning from her morning walk burst out, "Is everything okay?"

I ignored her comment and kept running. I surprised myself, wondering about how only the day before, I couldn't even walk. It seemed like all of my reflexes were connected to the fear of something happening to Mazen. It was a fear that drove me forward and gave me energy I never thought I possessed. I leaped over a pile of garbage and a broken stroller. I tripped, cut my knee and scrapped my chin raw. I ignored my pain, lifted myself as fast as I could, and continued to run with blood flowing down my leg.

The business was at the corner of a main highway, usually, a five-minute walk from my home that I believe I ran in less than a minute. There was a huge commotion surrounding the business. Passersby were peeking through the windows. I panicked.

A man yanked at my arm as I walked through the entrance and said, "Madame, I wouldn't go in there if I were you."

"But I own the business and my son is in there. Let go of me!" I replied, flinging his arm off me.

Frozen by what I'd seen, I collapsed and prayed they weren't going to shoot Mazen. Two men had him facing the wall with one rifle pressed at the center of his back and the other at his neck. Walid, a close friend of Mahmoud's and a neighboring business owner, stood in front of Mazen. He faced the intruders and said, "Shoot me instead. The boy is too young. He has a future ahead of him." Then, when he saw me, he added, "This is his mother. He's her only son. Please have mercy."

Then, a short and stocky militiaman looked at me and said, "Oh, I know who she is. We kidnapped this kid ten years ago, but unfortunately, we were ordered to return him. Now his father's dead and the only way we will let him go is if he never questions what we take from this place. We don't take much, but when we need teapots, teacups, and other miscellaneous items, we will take them."

"Not a problem. I will make sure that he never questions you again. In fact, I am willing to pay for whatever you need. But please, leave him alone." Walid rolled up his sleeves and signaled them to move their rifles away from Mazen.

My heart was beating against my chest and my temples throbbed as if someone were inviting me to unleash piercing screams and rivers of tears. A flood of electric current ran through my veins and my choking inhalations of air paralyzed my vocal cords, leaving me speechless. If the militiamen had asked for everything we had in the store at that moment, I would have surrendered all. Instead, they moved their rifles away from Mazen and jerked their bodies around. I watched the tall and thin invader slip his arm through the rifle sling and lay the rifle tight against his shoulder to make sure he had total control of the firing side. After looking at his face for a few seconds, I recognized him. He belonged to the People's Liberation Army, namely, the Progressive Socialist Party, whose headquarters was a block away from the business. He was also the same person who had barged into my husband's office when Mazen was fourteen, four years after they'd kidnapped him. I was sitting in the office chatting with Mahmoud when he broke into our conversation, seized Mazen's picture frame and said, "Nice kid." He didn't admit at the time that he was the one who was in charge of the kidnapping when Mazen was ten. He didn't touch Rania and Dania's pictures; he was interested only in Mazen. Mahmoud motioned me to leave. I walked away, frustrated and confused.

Now, five years later, I hoped he'd leave us alone, but instead, he lit a cigarette, took a deep puff, gave me the evil eye, and knocked a shelf full of crystal glassware onto the floor. "I will be back," he said.

I shook my legs for a few seconds to dislodge the tiny pieces of crystal from my feet, looked behind me to make sure he had left, and dashed toward Mazen. I reached up to wrap my arms around his tall stature, and soaked his shirt with tears of relief. The smell of his perspiration soared through my nostrils as an indication of relief and denouement. The business once known for its fine china and crystal became my *bête noir* or black beast, as the French would say. I wanted nothing more to do with it.

"Let's close for the day," I said, still holding onto Mazen.

"No, I'm staying here for a while. Walid saved my life and I want to show him my appreciation. You go home and I'll close up early this afternoon."

I looked at Walid. "No words can express my gratitude. Thank you."

I felt lost. I wasn't strong enough to tame the fear of death and to ask it to sit by me while I contemplated the universe to communicate secretly with God and to learn more about what He had in store for Mazen. I wasn't prepared to dismiss what had just happened and surrender Mazen to the whims of saboteurs and murderers. *How was I to take a chance that his attackers were not going to return or trust them to leave him alone?*

I did not want to comprehend the politics of a war-torn country and I certainly wasn't ready to lose a son to a group of murderous assailants. To me something serious was at stake if I were to remain in Lebanon. It was a matter of life or death. I wanted Mazen to live a free life, a life with unshackled thoughts. The last thing I wanted him to be around was the smell of mortality. Mazen had once told me how chilling it was to go to the hospital morgue to see his father stashed in a cold drawer as the men of the family were preparing to take him to the funeral home. He said he didn't like the smell of death, but that his uncle had requested that he retrieve his father's wedding band and watch before they left the hospital.

Dumbfounded by such a horrifying account, I hugged him. "In time, sweet memories will nullify such repulsive images and feelings, and the melodic memories of your father will be restored. I know how much you loved him and how painful it must be to live without him."

It was small comfort. But I wanted him to feel, smell, and taste the sweet flow of life through infinite compassion and love. I wanted to shield him from evil minds and nefarious criminals. I yearned for him to spend the rest of his life stimulated by the aroma of pleasantries, not the aroma of death or the breathless rhythm of sniper weaponries and assassins.

Chapter 5

The Green Line

The civil war in Lebanon lasted for fourteen years and claimed approximately 120,000 lives. Apolitical and tolerant of all religions during my tenure in Beirut, I coached my children to be the same. The two warring factions, Christians from the East and the Muslims from the West, each operated under the control of its corresponding militia leader. My neighbors were a diverse representation of Muslim Shia, Sunni, Druze, with a minority of Christian Maronites and Roman Catholics, who at the time, resisted religious adversity and the neat religious division of the population. The partition made no sense to them or even to many of the Muslims who also chose to defy the reigning political culture and retain their residence in East Beirut. By the time Mazen had become a teenager, he too took an impartial stance in the face of strong opposition and conservative ministries who had dictated the main divide.

We lived in West Beirut, five miles away from the "Green Line," a name derived from the verdure that grew in the abandoned space between both sides of the city. Snipers were always at work there.

The echoes of their sniper shots swept through nearby neighborhoods and made people wonder if greed caused the young snipers to relive a lost childhood and play war games, or if they were simply belligerent and trigger-happy. They sniped at the blowing grass to display their nocturnal power as the sun's rays penetrated the gloom of the night sky's withering anger.

I held Mazen's hand at the dinner table and reached deep for my words. "I made a serious decision this afternoon, a decision that I am going to execute no matter how you feel about it. Your sisters and I are going to help you pack this evening so that you can leave tomorrow at sunrise."

"What did you just say? Do you mean I'm leaving the country? Why didn't you talk to me first? Who told you it was safe to leave?"

"I spoke with Nouhad Said, my friend Marie Claude's mother, and asked for her help. Her leading position in the Lebanese government is to our advantage. She promised to send Marie Claude, who's staying with her for a while, to meet us at the other side of the Green Line."

"So now Marie Claude is involved? Why are we jeopardizing her life?"

"We're not jeopardizing her life. She knows how to handle herself. She will take us to the city of Jounieh seaport where I will stay with you until you board the cargo ship that will take you to Cyprus. From there, you will fly to the United States and stay with your grandparents until your sisters and I join you early this summer. I prepared your passport and purchased your ticket to Detroit. I am worried and I don't want to take any chances on the militia visiting with you again," I said, trying to catch my breath.

Mazen seemed as though his heart was ripped by the sudden realization that he was leaving us. He knit his brow while his eyes filled with tears. Our middle-aged Ethiopian housekeeper, Salam, who always shared her ancient tales each time she sensed the atmosphere was tense, was obsessed with baking. She set a plate of fresh bread in front of Mazen and suggested that he taste it. The aroma filled the air with the sweetness of her newly added ingredients—honey and flaxen seed. She saw eating fresh bread as a great occasion to break the disturbing silence that fell upon us at the dinner table after the announcement.

When he refused the bread, she took his hand, guided him to the front porch, and pointed to the new moon. His sisters and I followed. She said, "Mazen, what you see is the rebirth of the moon after its death. Think of yourself as the moon; this will not be the first or the last time that you will experience death and rebirth in life. I know that you feel like you are deserting your mother and sisters, but they will be safe. In time, you will learn to celebrate the new moons as they come and go with songs and tears of joy and to endure the bitter times and morbid moments in your life. Happier moments will prevail."

Dania ignored Salam's tale, put her hand on my arm and said, "Mama, how high is the grass at the Green Line? Are you sure that the snipers won't be firing at civilians in the morning?"

"The grass is very high. It's not as if we're being forced to march to our death. Many people who work for a living go back and forth every day. Also, Nouhad Said sent word to militia chieftains who oversee the Green Line to make sure they respect the morning ceasefire. There are stringent orders by both sides to ease the crossing of civilians who need to be on either side of the demarcation line for at least six hours a day. So far, there haven't been any fatalities. We could have waited a few weeks for the airport to re-open, but I fear the madness of the People's Liberation Army and I don't want to take a chance of losing your brother."

Mazen remained silent after listening to Salam, and on his way back to the kitchen, he stopped by the family room. His perturbation reflected in his face and was noticeable from across the room. He looked defeated. He held his father's picture and whispered, "Please tell me what to do. I don't want to leave Mama and my sisters alone. They need a man to protect them."

I, too, paused to contemplate the moonless night, but the smell of Mahmoud's death emerged out of the darkness and spoke to the hurricane of my fears. *He will be fine…*

Mahmoud's passing changed my primitive perception of death and gave me reason to believe that on a spiritual level, we can build a bridge between the living and the dead in order to communicate in unimaginable ways. I became accustomed to speaking to him because I believed that, even though he was physically absent, his spirit remained alive. His spirit remained animated in the aria of my mind and its energy gave me the psychological comfort I needed to move forward. It was the kind of comfort that is as colorless as the meaning of life itself but radiant in the temple of my mind.

We helped Mazen pack and I prepared a light bag to spend the night in Jbeil, a city not too far from Jounieh, so that I could watch him sail away from the hotel room's balcony.

By morning, I could not shut out the sound of Rania's and Dania's muffled cries and affectionate hugs. They had told me that they feared Mazen might perish at the Green Line. And because he had become a fatherly figure in their lives, the thought of losing him was devastating. I turned away from such a heartbreaking image and although I thought I could handle it, I was holding my breath.

Rania ran toward the chauffeur and said, "Please watch over them."

Reluctant to tell her that he was just dropping us off, he smiled and said, "Of course, I will."

We drove away shortly after sunrise.

"Stand in line, Madame, and wait until we call your name!" yelled the soldier at the crosspoint with a bold tone.

"Yes, sir," I replied obediently.

A few hours later, a man standing behind us panicked for whatever reason and raced away as though a wolf were pursuing him. No sooner had he disappeared behind the stationed military tank, we heard gunshots. I looked at Mazen and said, "Don't look back. Act like you didn't hear a thing."

I listened to the pounding of my heart and occasionally glanced at the soldiers' moves. I feared their wrath and when one of them stared at Mazen and me, I raised an eyebrow disdainfully and turned away.

Even though they were the ones carrying the weapons, I wasn't going to show them that I was afraid.

A few women standing down the line from me wept. One of them had a little boy whom she feared might break loose from her tight grip to follow the commotion. She raised her dress above her knees and squatted to speak to the boy with black and lustrous eyes and explain that he would be spanked if he didn't obey her.

I was nearly dizzy from heat and thirst from standing in the same place for over five hours. The commanding officer finally came from behind the tank that concealed the assassination and shouted, "Move, everyone, move quickly! I want all of you east of the Green Line in fifteen minutes or less."

I confess I had never been so frightened. *This was a mistake— except it was too late.*

For a moment, I felt rooted in the earth until Mazen looked back, grabbed my arm, recovered his footing, and hastened forward through five hundred yards of grass until we reached the edge of the road. We raised our eyes to the sky to thank the angels that lifted us to safety, and we walked over a path of flat stones that made our achievement seem like a crowning glory.

We turned around to find a shadowy place to stand until we saw Marie Claude. She too, was standing under the shade of a tree. Its light branches swayed with the wind, making an ordinary image seem picturesque. Startled by our presence after waiting for hours, she said, "Let's go straight to the Jounieh seaport. It's about one o'clock and the cargo ship is leaving at five this afternoon. We need to get there early and make sure they don't give up his spot."

We concurred and rushed to her car.

"By the way, Mazen, this isn't going to be fun. You will get a taste of what it's like to ride on Noah's Ark," she said with a faint smile that expressed tenderness.

"Well, that's good. I hope it's a sign that God will be merciful."

"Oh, you'll be fine. You know I don't believe in that stuff," she said as she rushed to her car.

The seaport was congested with young travelers, and merchants with their animal stock. It appeared, at least for the moment, that the innocence of these young lives was no longer a virtue, but a prison. Merciless war rats whose objective was to terrorize and feed upon the blood of the innocent to satisfy some temporary political fad had imprisoned them. Whether Christian or Muslim, you were bound to be preyed upon by someone who thought you threatened his political cradle.

I looked at Marie Claude and said, "The only thing that is emerging out of this civil war is a country torn by grief, and children gutted of life's treasures and distraught by war's casualties."

She curled me around and said, "Don't let me get started!"

By five-thirty in the afternoon, the shipmaster authorized passengers to board the cargo ship. He stood facing them and said, "Place all important papers in a plastic bag because we may be subject to stormy weather. If you don't have any, we will provide you with one once you board the ship. We may not have enough benches, so some of you can take turns sitting or standing alongside the animals until we reach Larnaca, Cyprus. You also have the option to sit on your bags or the floor, but I don't recommend it since it is usually damp. It will take us about five to six hours to get there. Do you have your papers?"

As if orchestrated, all passengers snapped up their papers and bags and prepared to embark the ship. For a while, my silence throbbed with pain and I wasn't sure whether I should be weeping or celebrating. The ship was dazzling in the setting sun and the aquamarine seawater reflected against the red and white Plimsoll mark lines on the side of the ship. I felt like my heart was going to rise out of me, but I took control of my emotions, walked over to Mazen, and said, "You are going to be just fine. I will stick around for the night so that I can keep a close eye on the ship from my hotel room. Not that I can do anything, but sometimes, gazing at the ocean is the way to peace of heart and mind. I love you. Now, give me a tight hug. May God be with you."

He walked away with his head tilted and his eyes focused on the dirt road ahead of him.

Marie Claude and I rushed to the hotel, took the elevator to the fifth floor, and walked out to the balcony to stare at the drifting grace of the red and white lines of the ship as it made its way north toward Larnaca. I waved at its drenching shadow as it darkened and merged behind the waves.

Chapter 6

Bitterness at the Courthouse

Mazen and I had become very close after his father died, and his friendship was invaluable. We comforted each other during moments of need. We stuck together through the stormy tides of life and came to shore holding hands and smiling that we made it through. When I was down or feeling sorry for myself for being a widow, struggling to find a job and raise three teenagers, he'd lift my spirits and tell me that he would drop out of school and find a job if he must. If I ever got upset with him for driving too fast, getting tickets, and adding to my expenses, he would lower his head and say, "I'm sorry. How can I make it up to you?"

I didn't ever find the need to ground him during his childhood because he never repeated the same mistake twice. I couldn't get angry with him, at least no longer than I would with myself because he always made it easy for me to forgive him.

From the day Mazen was born, I feared that something might happen to him. My mother once commented, "Leave him alone. Let him ride the bike up and down the block by himself. You don't have to run to keep up with him! Nothing is going to happen to him. He'll never grow to become a confident young man if you keep this up. You are scaring all of us."

"Ma, I have a feeling that something is going to happen to him. I don't know why, but I've felt this way since the day he was born."

On July 24, 1999, a day after I'd had a dream about some lady wanting me to take a black snake from her, we celebrated Mazen's thirty-first birthday at Buddy's Pizza on Michigan Avenue in Dearborn. I arrived at the restaurant satisfied that I was going to be with my children and grandchildren. It was a warm day. The sun was laboring heavily in the sky even though in the morning, the weather forecast had predicted the onset of a rainy afternoon. Once I parked, I prayed that the spirit of hope in nature would turn all my worries into good thoughts. I hoped that the glistening sun beaming across the hood of my car would clear the air and make this day one to remember.

My daughters Rania and Dania arrived the same time that I did. Mazen, who had arrived before all of us, had already parked. He was carrying his infant son Jemail in his arms while his wife Mona was opening the stroller. Mazen placed Jemail in the stroller, unbuckled Mahmoud from his car seat, made sure Mona didn't need any help, then held Yasmine's hand, carrying Mahmoud with his other arm and walking with a father's pride into the restaurant. I enjoyed watching him display the characteristics of a caring and loving father, but I noticed he wasn't wearing his usual smile. At first, I panicked, but then I released my fear by assuming his stoic comportment might have something to do with the pressure of working full-time and taking three college classes.

The smell of pizza wafted through the air, tempting me to forget about my diet and eat more than just a salad. Once seated, Mazen looked at me briefly and smiled. His smile seemed generated out of respect for me more than out of the comfort of his mind and soul. He didn't have his usual strength, stamina, and alertness, and he barely concentrated on any of the conversations that were going on between his sisters and among the rest of us. I glanced at him and questioned him with my eyes. He raised his hand and gave me the *"I'm fine"* signal.

I placed the birthday cake at the corner of the table to keep it out of the way and walked over to whisper in his ear, "I love you."

Again, he gave me a fake smile and said, "I love you too."

Mazen waved the waitress down and explained to her that his children were hungry and that he wanted fast service. I was suspicious, but I thought that perhaps he was tired and he wasn't too happy about turning thirty-one. I wished him health and happiness after dinner, as we were getting ready to watch him blow out the candles. I smiled. We hugged for a brief moment; I patted him on the shoulder as a sign of pride and looked at his children, who were waiting eagerly for a piece of cake.

Why God tests us with what we treasure the most, I'll never know, but I will never stop trying to understand. A few months prior to Mazen's birthday, he'd had headaches and, if he stopped by on weekends, he'd frequently ask for an aspirin or Tylenol. My usual comment would be, "Why does a young man your age have a headache in the morning? Have you seen a doctor about this?" His response was always, "Just give me the pills and don't worry about me."

His wife Mona called me the day after his birthday and said in a piercing voice,

"I need help in convincing Mazen to see a doctor. He's not sleeping at night! He wakes up clutching his head with his hands asking me to give him something to take away his headache."

With a knot in my stomach, I said, "I will do my best to get him to see a doctor."

I put the receiver down and began to reflect upon the infinite causes of his headaches and my recent dream. Could it be cancer again? Wasn't losing his father to cancer enough? The thought of Mazen having cancer was like a fist to the stomach. *No…it can't be. Not again. Not my family.*

I picked up the phone and after a multitude of attempts, spoke with Mazen. I'm not sure if it was the seriousness in my voice or the inner fear that he was experiencing that led him to say, "Okay Mom. I'll see a doctor this afternoon."

Content that Mazen had finally agreed to see a doctor to unveil the mystery of his headaches, Mona joined him to see his primary care physician. I waited patiently at home, debating whether to jump in the car and follow them or to sit tight and hope that I wouldn't be swept away by premature grief.

The phone rang. "Hi. It's Mona. The doctor said that even though his headaches could be caused by severe stress or a tumor, he wanted him to be seen by an optometrist before he could prescribe a Magnetic Resonance Imaging (MRI)."

"What are you talking about? Am I hearing things? Tumor?" I screamed.

"I want him to forego the vision test and go directly for an MRI, but his doctor said that he couldn't justify it. What does he mean?" she said.

"Maybe because it's an expensive test and the insurance company won't pay for it until they can prove that it is necessary? I don't know…" I answered.

Mona drove Mazen to see the optician, who found a swollen optic nerve. He suggested an immediate MRI. I panicked. I could not tolerate the thought of MRI without thinking "cancer."

Mazen was never the aggressive type. He played quietly with his friends throughout his life. His teachers reported excellent conduct on his report cards and he was hardworking and reliable. When I signed him up for karate at the age of ten, he came home from his first practice, went into his room, locked the door behind him, and cut his karate outfit into pieces. When I asked him why, he said, "I hate violence! I will never play karate again."

I walked away and thought, *I should have asked him first before signing him up or buying the clothes.* As much as Mazen tried to stay away from trouble, trouble came after him.

Despite my emotional struggles, I felt fear and anger. I wanted to be alone. I wanted to scream. I couldn't focus or tend to my one-year-old son Adam's needs. Ernie read my distress and took full charge of Adam. My desire for solitude increased. I wanted to be alone where I could talk to myself, ask myself questions and rationalize desirable responses. Talking to myself when my mind is stuck in mud is like smoking a cigarette and puffing out peace signals. I had hoped that the rage within me would dissipate, but instead, it haunted me throughout the evening.

Suddenly, I had a great vital thought, an inspiration. I knew that this time, if I began my prayers, God would intervene and make sure that nothing negative would come my way. I had renegotiated a peace treaty with Him after five years of turning away from prayer. I was mad at Him for deserting me when Mahmoud died, but, after years of reading books and consulting with religious leaders, I had discovered the rationality of death, or at least I thought I had.

The next day, I tried not to think of the MRI. If something were wrong, Mazen would have had more than just headaches. It was my understanding at the time that people who had brain tumors would have seizures—and Mazen had had none.

As hard as I tried, I couldn't stop the sound of Indian war drums from pounding in my head. I sat on the edge of my bed, closed my eyes, and began to meditate. I started my meditation by disciplining myself to think positive. *Why worry? Mazen's fine. He's healthy and the worst thing he ever did to hurt his body was to smoke. Yes, smoking is bad and his father died of lung cancer, but that didn't mean that he was going to die too. Don't think about tumors. The MRI will show nothing and the doctors are going to send him home. Take your mind off Mazen. Convert your fear into energy, and do some major housecleaning. Look for a baby-sitter for Adam . . .* I stood up, ended my meditation and set aside my desire to know the unknown. I dismissed negative thoughts, and allowed the world to illuminate me.

Midday sun warmed the living room as its brightness seeped through the translucent curtains that decorated the picture windows of my family, living, and dining rooms. But the curtains appeared gray and dusty.

I darted to the garage, seized the ladder, and held it over the white marbled tile, positioning it firmly between the couch and the window. Carefully mounting each step, I reached the height of the rods and prepared to grasp the hooks and remove the sheers until I looked across the distance and froze at the sight of the sun twinkling over the tops of trees and climbing into the sky.

My yard backed to a ravine where the Rouge River dropped to a hillside bank congested with trees. Even though I wanted to lift the heavy shroud from my head, I couldn't. I thought of spirituality. I thought of God and the heavens, and whether He would listen to me if I cried for guidance. Life, love, and relationships became less meaningful to me as I pondered the potential ruins of happiness. I believed in God, but I didn't feel linked to Him. I wanted to become friends with Him. I had depended on Him to lift me from the pains of past relationships, but I didn't feel genuinely connected with Him. Dependency and connectivity are very different and I was yearning for the latter. I hoped to maintain my dependency on Him so that He could help me conquer my fears, but I wanted to feel His presence. I wanted to carry on imagined conversations with Him to feel that He was within me, as the unborn lies connected to his mother through an umbilical cord. I knew that if anything bad were to happen to Mazen, I would feel incompetent as a mother. I believed that because I brought him into this world, it was my responsibility to keep him in it.

I took down the curtains, washed them on the delicate cycle, and placed them carefully over the backyard fence to dry in the sun. I walked back into the house and realized that the power had gone out. It was around 4:00 in the afternoon. It had been a hot summer and the sound of air conditioners was blasting through the neighborhood. I assumed this was a temporary outage caused by electricity overload. I plugged in my landline phone to call Detroit Edison to report the problem. The message at the other end of the line promised that the problem would be fixed within a few hours. Unfortunately, that was untrue. I'm not sure if the electric company even knew what had happened. I assembled my candles and supplies, hoping that the electricity would come back within an hour or so. I unplugged my computer and refrigerator and kept the radio on for updated information. I lit a candle in every room and hoped for the power to return.

The phone rang. It was Mona. Panicky and overwhelmed, she screamed, "Now what? Mazen's MRI is scheduled for six o'clock this evening. There's no power in the entire state! They think it may take days before the power comes back. What do I do?"

She was right. The blackout lasted for four consecutive days. It was a combination of lack of maintenance, human error, and equipment failures. The outage affected large portions of the Midwest and Northeast United States and Ontario, Canada.

"Proceed to the radiologist and, if he doesn't have a generator, he will recommend a hospital that does. Would you like me to take him?" I said calmly.

"No, I can handle this!" she exclaimed.

Mona's fear provoked suspicion all over again and I sat at the kitchen table to sort out my thoughts. To avoid falling back into wariness, I re-centered my thoughts on finding a babysitter for Adam. He was a year old and his father and I both worked full-time. The nanny who had been watching him had fallen ill and I knew that it was going to be hard to find someone I could trust again.

I picked up the phone to put the word out among friends and family. I began by calling my daughter Rania to ask if she knew anyone who might watch Adam from September to May. Divorced and jobless, she was living alone with her two-year-old son, Malik.

"Don't worry about finding a sitter. I'll watch Adam when you go back to work, but I have a question. Can you watch Malik when you get home in the afternoon? I want to go back to school to become a teacher. I need seventy additional credit hours. My advisor at Wayne State doesn't believe that I can use any of my credits from my Master's in Business Administration. It might take me a couple of years, but by then, Malik will be ready for preschool and Adam for daycare. What do you think?"

I placed my lips close to the receiver to make sure she heard me and said with enthusiasm, "It sounds like a great plan. I'm glad that you're willing to watch Adam and yes, I will watch Malik. By the way, can we try this out tomorrow morning? I promised your Aunt Samerah that I would interpret a case for her in court since I'm off this summer," I stated.

"Are you a certified interpreter?" she asked.

"Oh yes. It was part of my doctoral program in education. Even though I don't use my certification for a living, I enjoy helping your Aunt Samerah out every now and then. It'll take about an hour."

"Of course, bring him any time. I'll be home all day."

I hung up and pranced with delight. *Who would be better to watch Adam than his sister? All is good...at least, for the moment.*

Early the next morning, to make sure I was in court by 9:00 a.m., I buckled Adam in his car seat and drove over to Rania's. The power was still out, but my sister told me that the case was still on since the courthouse used a generator. I hugged Adam, gave Rania a hurried kiss on the cheek, and rushed to the 19th District Court in Dearborn.

While sitting quietly in the courtroom waiting for the judge, who happened to be my mother's friend, I became restless. I fidgeted with my paperwork and looked around the courtroom. Then, I noticed my mother's face pressed against the transparent glass of the courtroom door. What was my mother doing here? Was she coming to see her judge friend? No, that was impossible since she was handling the case I was interpreting. Then, I noticed my daughter Dania standing motionless behind her. Her eyes were wide with terror. As my mother quietly opened the door, a hot rush of blood pulsated almost instantly to my head. I pressed my fingers against my temples to suppress the throbbing discomfort, stood up, and ran toward her.

"Why are you here?" I asked as I walked her out of the courtroom.

Trying to hide her fear, my mother said, "The results of Mazen's MRI are back and his doctor is driving him to the hospital as we speak..."

That's all she had to say before my knees buckled under me. I dropped to the ground and screamed, "No! The radiologist made a mistake. Something's wrong. He misread Mazen's MRI!"

A court officer ran toward us. He pulled me up and said, "Leave this courthouse now! Take your problems home!" I yanked my arm from him and walked away.

His insensitive words deepened my wounds and brought me back to reality. Dania explained to him what was happening, but he ignored her, walked behind me, and mumbled, "You're leaving, right?" I looked back and ignored him.

Dania held onto my arm, cried, and begged me to think positive. *Of course, I thought to myself...positive, positive. I need to think positive. How can I? How could I see light in a brain tumor? Where would I get the strength and energy I needed to pull through this? God, please help me! I need your guidance now!*

Out in the parking lot, I told my mother that I needed to be with Mazen at the hospital.

"Of course... I'll drive," she said.

"No, no. I will."

I knew that if I was going to see Mazen, I needed to be strong and by holding onto the steering wheel, I could stay focused. Yet, once behind the wheel, I realized that it was impossible to stay focused. My mind drifted into an unknown world, a world I had never seen or thought of before. I felt lost in a wood as though standing in a labyrinth, struggling to find my way. Images of Mazen's terrified face rushed through the strange quiet of my mind. I couldn't stop myself from imagining what he went through when he learned of his diagnosis. He loved his wife and children and I'm sure the painful and raw news threw him into a state of panic.

The climate of my life changed as I scoured for portents that could help prepare me for what lay ahead but could think of none. I feared my agonizing encounter and felt helpless.

Then I thought...*what am I going to say to Mazen? What am I going to do?*

By the time we walked up to the neurology department, I was out of breath. Nauseated by the smell of antiseptics and the trays of tasteless food that filled the air, I felt weak.

On my way to the family waiting room, I saw my cousin Nadia wheeling her seven-year-old daughter Natalie, diagnosed with terminal stomach cancer. She called my name. She looked at me inquisitively and said, "What are you doing here?"

"Oh, I'm not sure yet," I exclaimed, "but I'm in a hurry and I'll catch up with you later."

"Of course, I understand," she replied and continued her route. I'm sure she was puzzled, but I wasn't ready to talk to a mother about my fears when she was already going through the fear of losing her own daughter. My own safeguard against explaining anything to her was blurry and at the time, seemed unnecessary.

I wasn't sure what to expect when I walked into the waiting room. I looked around and saw Linda, Mazen's mother-in-law, waiting patiently.

"Mazen and Mona are still with the doctor," she said as she handed me his MRI report.

I saw an empty seat in the corner of the waiting room and collapsed into it. I began to read. I didn't understand all of the medical terms, but I gathered that his chances of survival were slim. My hands trembled. I could no longer deny the horrifying reality of Mazen's illness with science violently spreading the scent of death in my mind. Dania laid her head on my shoulder and moaned, "I love Mazen. I love him so much, Ma…"

"I know you do. I know…" I wrapped my arms tightly around her and prayed that our tears were not the beginning of a storm of agonizing struggles.

Mazen came out holding Mona's hand. Mona yanked her hand out of his, began crying and waving her arms in despair. Mazen pulled her toward him, hugged her tight, looked her in the eyes and said intently, "Stop crying. I'm going to be fine." He then saw me from the corner of his eye, straightened his back and said, "Don't worry Ma. I'm going to be just fine."

I hugged him firmly to maintain my balance from the ground shifting beneath me as surely as an earthquake. I thought about the way Mazen always carried himself. He had a lot of respect for himself and a concern to please others. His presence always seemed to fill the atmosphere with love and anyone who knew him, knew him for life. Good-natured, he pardoned everyone and anything. He was like a flower that scattered its seeds to make the world a better place. I'm sure he was hurting and shocked by the unpredictable illness, but he was still able to spread the fruit of peace by encouraging me not to worry.

Mona cried in rage, "No you're not! The doctor said you have two weeks! He told you to go home and write your will!"

I was appalled. What I had tried not to believe had established itself across the room. Tormented, I was refusing to accept the ugly truth, but Mona's words were like wavering torches among the dead. She, too, was hurting. I had to think quickly. There was no time to dwell on negative thoughts. I had to store up positive energy and take action.

I gathered my composure, turned toward Mona and asked her calmly, "What happened? Please start from the beginning."

With a quivering voice, she murmured, "His doctor called in the morning to let us know that his MRI results were in. He asked us to meet him in his office. Once we got there, he told us that Mazen needed to see a neurologist as soon as possible. He saw how weak we both were and offered to drive. Immediately upon our arrival there, he spoke with the neurologist and left. . . Am I living a nightmare? Please do something!"

I lowered my head and reached for a hankie from the tissue box near the magazine rack. I wiped away my tears, straightened my posture, and told her in a very serious tone, "You're right. This is all a nightmare. None of it is true. The report has been misinterpreted. We're going to put a cap on this and put an end to this doctor's illusion of control."

I walked over to the corner of the room and prayed that would God give me strength to offer Mazen the same support. I wanted to confirm to both him and myself that we were going to get through this as we did all the restless and dark moments of our lives. We were all suffering, but he was certainly more distressed than any of us. The road to recovery would be like climbing a broken ladder, but my soul charged me to travel with the light of hope and give Mazen a set of wings to fly again. I didn't want him to suffer or dwell on his diagnosis. I didn't want him to go round and round, tiring himself with negative energy or squeezing himself dry and helping the disease along. I wanted him to trust in the golden rays of sunlight that radiated against his face as he stood facing the afternoon sun, gathering the warmth behind his scarlet tears to serve as a bridge between God's heaven and his earthly fears.

Chapter 7

The Radiance of Doubt

Mazen had been diagnosed with an *inoperable brain tumor*. I knew I had a storm ahead of me and I was only marginally prepared. The oncologist ordered a biopsy. I wondered if the biopsy was even necessary, especially after he had told Mazen that he only had two weeks to live. Also, my readings revealed that there was no conclusive evidence that a biopsy could cause cancer cells to spread, but I feared that it might.

I walked away from my computer. I stopped talking to my medical doctor friends and I put a halt on research. I wanted to be among the ignorant. It felt like the wind of a hurricane was running through my body. Sometimes reading about an illness can cause more grief than relief. When eighteenth-century poet Thomas Gray coined the term "Where ignorance is bliss" in a passage from "On a Distant Prospect of Eton College," I'm sure he knew that excessive knowledge could be confusing and emotionally detrimental. Yes, "knowledge is power" but at that moment in my life, reading a few stories, online studies, or medical journals wasn't going to give me the power I needed to make a difference in the outcome of Mazen's illness.

I was nervous about the request, especially when I saw the odd expression of Mazen's eyes the night before. I didn't say anything. Then, I thought, *why would the doctor tell Mazen that he had two weeks to live and still request a biopsy? Could he be in doubt of the diagnosis? Is it possible that he misinterpreted the MRI?*

While at the hospital and waiting for the nurses to roll Mazen through the long and narrow corridor of the surgical unit to perform a biopsy, I stood next to him, wondering *who was going to benefit from the procedure—Mazen or the hospital?* He lay on the pre-op bed that was too small for a man of his stature and clutched my hand. He hoped to find *hope* while living under a death sentence. His wife, Mona, sat on the other side of his bed, a rosebud that had lost its petals to an early spring frost. We were both motionless. The air felt heavy and oppressive.

Mazen whispered, "Mama, I feel like a number. Look at the patients around me. We are like grumbling cattle awaiting our turn to be slaughtered. Do I have to do this?"

I ignored his question. "Maybe they put everyone in the same area because they're running out of space." My words orbited the room like a toneless requiem.

Mazen arched his eyebrows and turned his face. I didn't think anything I said would make him feel better. He was in a dark tunnel, longing for relief.

The nurse walked toward him. "Your turn, young man. Are you ready?"

Mona clenched her jaw, and I struggled to remain calm and hold back my tears. My goal was to give Mazen hope when hope was out of sight. We yearned for someone to tell us that this was all a mistake and that Mazen had been falsely diagnosed. With a firm grip, my hands trembled. I was trying not to make truce with his illness. On the contrary, I was prepared to fight it with every ounce of strength I had left.

"Let's wait outside, Mona. The nurse said that he'd be back in about two hours and that we'd get the results in two days. Do you want a cup of coffee?" My voice resonated in every direction and framed itself around her tightened visage. We walked out of the surgical unit waiting for *hope.*

Two hours later, Mazen came out of surgery with fear caught in his throat. He said nothing. His eyes maneuvered around the room, laboriously trying to figure out where he was. An hour later, he rose from his bed, dressed and prepared himself for the longest two days of his life.

The next morning, I gathered the little strength that I had and called Mazen's family doctor to inform him that once the biopsy results were in, I wanted a second opinion. He was speechless for a moment and then said, "Of course. I understand. I will email you the names of several doctors whom I know we can trust. They work out of a hospital in Detroit."

I thanked him, stared at the receiver, turned it over a few times in my hand, and wondered whether the dryness of the doctor's voice and his reluctance to respond quickly to my request indicated that he, too, believed Mazen was terminal. I flung the receiver across the room, ran to my bedroom, stretched across the bed and buried my tears in the deep crevices of my pillow.

Three days later, Mona phoned to let me know that she had the biopsy results. She invited me over to read them. Mazen was diagnosed with a primary anaplastic astrocytoma grade III, one of the worst and fastest growing brain tumors. He sat quietly across the room as I read the report. I looked at him briefly to see his reaction, but quickly turned away when I saw tears streaming down his cheeks. I stared back at the paper to act as though I were still reading, but I needed time to think and I didn't want Mazen to see my face or read my apprehension.

It's just words on paper. Many people had been riddled with cancer and now they are well. If it can happen to them, then why can't it be true for Mazen? I had read many reports and popular books that substantiated miraculous recoveries when his father took ill. There had been many cases in which the well-established diagnosis left no hope for treatment, yet terminal patients lived years beyond their medical diagnosis; either the disease was cured or lay dormant for many years. Renowned medical communities might dispute such views for lack of scientific evidence, but I still believed that I could do something to extend Mazen's life. I didn't want Mazen to give up and die when I knew that there was a slight possibility to change the course of his journey. Numerous success stories were listed on the National and American Brain Tumor websites.

Such stories are often dismissed by conventional medicine because what some medical doctors fail to take into account is the belief that the body itself can play a significant role in the healing process. If we supported Mazen with love and showed him the potential to rejuvenate life-affirming possibilities, he might find reason to defy science and terminal predictions. I wanted him to reconnect with his soul and triumph over the lethal and voiced opinions of doctors who saw no hope in treating his tumor. I wanted him to smell the odor of getting well by using his body's natural ability to heal. It could all be mythical, but no one can deny that a positive attitude can reduce the harmful effects of stress on the body and possibly extend one's life.

I stood up and shouted, "Listen, Mazen! I don't want you ever to believe what you see on paper. I know that there are times when science has been proven wrong. Many researchers and osteopathic physicians have proven that it's all in the mind."

I wanted him to believe that he could revert to alternative treatments in order to heal. He could challenge medicine by using natural drugs or even religion. We could invite friends and family to join us in prayer at the mosque and with the right diet, and the fundamental belief that he could heal himself, nothing negative would happen to him.

He looked at me and said, "Ma, tell me what you want me to do so that I can get rid of this!" His teary eyes and droopy arms were an affirmation that he was going to make a conscious effort to fight the disease.

I stood frozen for a moment and said, "No, Mazen. It's not what I want you to do. It's what *you* are convinced you need to do. You must believe in what I am telling you in order to rid yourself of this diagnosis."

I turned to Mona whose face was pale with distress. "Mona, I rarely visit your home. I left it up to you to visit me when you found time, but now that Mazen's diagnosis is serious, you are going to see a lot more of me. I hope that you will welcome me in your home and allow me to share in all major decisions relating to Mazen's health."

"Of course! I'm too overwhelmed and I can't think straight even if I wanted to! Please do what you think is best. You are always welcome in my home. You can live here if you wish."

I reached out, hugged her tightly, and whispered in her ear, *"Together, we will win this battle."*

I knew she was hurting with the realization that her seven-year empire was beginning to tumble. She feared losing her husband, her partner, and the father of her young children. Her teary eyes spoke to me as she walked to and from the kitchen and the living room. She must have been looking for a sign of hope, raising her eyes and wondering if God would listen to her as she yearned for His mercy.

We spoke at length about mind over body, and she promised that she would encourage Mazen to defy science and triumph over his crisis. Mazen had told me that they had a strong bond, and I noticed that it became even stronger after his diagnosis. Mona held his hand and rubbed her cheeks against his arms at every opportunity. It was as if a sensory stimulus encountered by the diagnosis "you have two weeks to live" was immediately and irreversibly, embossed onto her brain. She possessed a powerful intuition, and I hoped that as his wife and confidante, she would convince him to pry into his inner strength and recover. We walked forth in the dark.

Mazen had met Mona for the first time when she was visiting with his sister Rania during the summer of 1992. He was working in Philadelphia at one of my brother Sammy's pizzerias when he decided to come home for a few days. He told me that he was lonely and that he was ready to marry if he found the right girl. I told him to take his time and to follow his heart. Miracles happen all the time. I must have spoken too soon. We were sitting on the side porch chatting and drinking coffee when Mona and her sister Susie drove up and walked past us to visit with Rania. Mazen raised his eyes as he stared at Mona and said, "Who is she? She's gorgeous!"

I smiled and said, "Looks like your desire to settle might already be in the making. That's Mona. She's my friend Linda Chami's daughter. We grew up together in the South end of Dearborn."

"Well, can I make arrangements to see more of her?"

"Of course," I said, wondering if *love at first sight* was what placed such a huge smile upon his face.

"Her grandfather just passed away. If you talk to *Umo* (Uncle) Mohamed, my brother-in-law, he would be more than willing to take you over there. This will give you a chance to see what her family is like and whether Mona is someone you want to pursue. If you get serious, we'll talk to her parents. What do you think?" He jumped at the idea.

"Can I go tonight?"

Carried away by the rushing breeze of a soft wind across my face, I couldn't stop smiling.

Chapter 8

The Ugly Face of Medicine

Mona called to inform me that per the oncologist's request, she'd scheduled an appointment with the neurologist. The night before we saw the doctor, I prepared a letter in which I described Mazen's experience with cancer. I ask him to be sensitive.

Once at the hospital and moments after the receptionist directed us to the examination room, the neurologist arrived. He entered the room and introduced himself. He was about six-feet-four, like Mazen, and had an aging posture and black suspenders. I looked at him with despair, and gave him the unsealed envelope titled "Please read privately."

He set it aside, flung Mazen's x-rays on a laminator view box slightly below the ceiling and pointed to each x-ray, explaining that the disease was quite advanced. Mazen nudged Mona and whispered something in her ear. They continued to whisper and glance at the x-rays. Then, they became silent.

The doctor proceeded to his desk, opened the letter, and began to read it aloud.

My son lost his father to lung cancer a few years ago and he is afraid. The oncologist who referred you to us told him that he had two weeks to live. I believe in the power of mind over body and that our inner voices can play a powerful role in the healing process. I'm not willing to think "terminal" and I'm determined to carry hope. I want you to help my son find his inner strength and spirituality and to lend him a helping hand, not a death sentence...

Upon hearing the contents of the letter, Mazen sighed deeply and said, "Mom...? How could you?"

By then, I'd lost patience. I stood up, faced the doctor whose reading voice was so emphatic and strident and said, "How many brain tumor patients have you treated thus far?"

"About three thousand," he replied with an expression that seemed to say, *"Why are you asking me this?"*

I looked at Mazen and Mona and said, "May I take charge here?"

"Of course," they replied almost simultaneously.

"Doctor, you walked into this room, introduced yourself, threw my son's x-rays in the view box and told him in a semi-civil tone that there was essentially *no hope*. Do you even know my son's name? If you do, I didn't hear you say it. You might have treated three thousand brain tumor patients, but I'm here trying to help one, and the *one* happens to be my son. If you are using Mazen to add his diagnosis and treatment to your future publications, you might want to add your next patient because we are leaving."

The doctor was speechless. We left his office vowing never to return. I walked ahead of Mazen and Mona to avoid showing my anger and to give myself time to think. I needed time to plan my next move.

As we exited the hospital, I looked at the glass doors ahead of me and sensed a flurry of negative images pulled my emotions in every direction. I hoped that I wasn't making a mistake by walking out of one of the so-called renowned hospitals in the country. I wanted a doctor whose primary concern was his patient, not his publications. *But how could I be making a mistake? They wrote him off anyway!*

Faced with losing Mazen, the father of three beautiful children, I felt helpless and betrayed. I wasn't asking for a miracle but for sensitivity. Family members of cancer patients' feelings are legitimate and they need to be honored. As a mother, my desire to die in his place was comparable to his will to live. I assured Mazen that I was going to find a doctor who would promise him life and joy. I wasn't going to let doctors execute his will to live in the medical arena, when the prayers oscillating beneath my eyelids gave me hope that he might live. I needed a patch of sunlight in a world that seemed cruel and cold.

The next day, upon the recommendation of my husband Ernie's uncle Robert, an emergency room physician. I drove Mazen to a hospital in Detroit. We met with a team of doctors: a surgeon, a radiologist, and a neurologist. I prayed that they would be a fresh source of hope rather than a tempest of despair.

After careful observation of the MRI films, the team looked at us and drifted into the back room.

I was fidgety. The laws of medical protocol blurred in my mind. The pain of truth pressed in. I looked at Mazen and Mona and said, "I'll be right back."

I joined the doctors in their private meeting and addressed the surgeon. "Can you help me?"

He turned around, put his arms around my shoulder and whispered, "I would have tried surgery and immunotherapy treatment, but the tumor has spread around the left hemisphere and it appears to be too large an area to operate on without damaging Mazen's language centers."

I was flooded with guilt, thinking how I had failed Mazen. He surrendered his trust to me when he first learned about his brain tumor and asked for my guidance. I had hoped that the surgeon would turn my streams of tears into rivers of joy, but instead, my eyes were bruised and swollen. I clenched my fists, took a deep breath and said, "But you're a renowned surgeon. You came highly recommended. Please don't tell me there's *no hope*."

"I am sorry, but there is none." The other two doctors who were listening to our conversation turned around and left the room.

My anger arose like a flame. I didn't know whether to explain to Mazen what I had just heard or to remain silent. I wiped away my tears, straightened my posture, and walked back to the front office. The surgeon followed me. My footsteps were heavy. My heart was heavier.

"Mazen, Mona, the surgeon is going to study the x-rays, and call us in a few days."

I looked at the surgeon and whispered, "It is just language. *Hope* is better than *hopelessness.*" We shook his hand and left.

I fretted and worried about Mazen. *The tumor had spread to the left side his brain?* I had researched the brain when I wrote my dissertation on memory, retention, and neuroscience, and learned that brain tumors can leave speech intact and its functions can shift to adjoining areas of the brain. *I wished I'd majored in medicine...*I tried to untangle the implications of what his surgeon had said and decided to meet with another brain surgeon to discuss the implications of surgery.

Two days after our visit with the medical team, and before I had a chance to visit with a third brain surgeon, Mazen's headaches became unendurably brutal. Mona called screaming, "I need help."

I hurried over. We called 911 and rushed him to emergency. I paged the neurologist and asked him to meet us in the emergency room. The neurologist looked at Mazen, examined his optic nerves to see if his blood vessels were compressed. He looked at Mona and said, "Let's keep him here for a while." He was diagnosed on July 29, and hospitalized on August 9, 1999.

While at the hospital, I hoped that the bitter truth of his diagnosis was a mistake. I couldn't stop thinking of the averted faces of his doctors when they informed us there was nothing they could do for Mazen, while withholding what they knew would happen before his death. Mona and I succumbed to the fierce pressure of accepting his hospitalization, though we feared the hidden mysteries of his brain tumor's manifestations.

While at the hospital, Mazen's illness had changed the pattern of our lives and a hospital was no longer a safe haven or refuge for cures and therapies, but a sheltered rainfall of bricks and stones. We were frightened by the doctors and nurses who gave us little opportunity to brainstorm for solutions, allowing us only ample regret to prepare for his impending death.

What is a brain tumor? I tried so hard to understand the medical jargon and make sense of the insensible, but my brain was shackled to the fatigued neurons that had once served as its nourishment. I reached out to my soul to ask what I could do to rid Mazen of his tumor, but it remained silent.

Mazen asked that one of us be with him at all times so, Mona and I set up a hospital schedule. We agreed that I would be with him late evenings, nights, and early mornings, and she'd take over late mornings, afternoons, and early evenings.

Unfortunately, Mazen's headaches were getting worse by the day and the doctors were arresting his pain with morphine. His room was large enough to welcome family members and friends, but I wasn't sure Mazen wanted them to watch his pitiful suffering. Neither did I want to deal with anyone who believed Mazen was going to die or who would approach him with a negative frame of mind. Frustrated at times by prolonged visits, I'd try to reduce my tension by looking out the window to observe the lagging sunlight filter its way through the smeary glass and land at the edge of Mazen's bed. It brought me peace. I prayed for mercy.

One morning, I pulled my chair close to Mazen's bed and held his hand. "Mazen, I love you, and I am not giving up. I will do everything I can to liberate you from your pain."

But then, I asked myself...*How? What can I do?* I journeyed in to the attic of my mind to search for options. I felt like an idiot in a room full of Einsteins. Or like sitting on a bare island in the middle of the ocean where rescue teams were absorbed by violent tides.

Mazen yanked his hand away from me and screamed from increased cranium pressure, "My head! I can't take this anymore."

The nursing assistant, who appeared to be in her mid-twenties, came rushing in. Startled, since I didn't see Mazen push the buzzer, I stared at her broad shoulders and white hospital uniform and wondered what she was going to do. She had given him a morphine injection about an hour earlier and I knew that it was too soon to give him another. My eyes followed her every move. She reached into her bulging pocket to retrieve a needle.

"What are you doing?" I asked.

The tone of my voice must have alarmed her. Somewhat hesitant, she spoke with an insolent smile, "Oh...I'm giving him a shot—doctor's orders."

"Excuse me, but are those morphine injections bulging out of your pocket?

"Yes."

"Are they for my son?"

"Yes, they are."

"Then take your hand out of your pocket and leave this room immediately. I will talk to the doctor myself about this. What makes you think that you can come in here and inject him with this potent opiate drug that can potentially kill him? A large overdose can cause asphyxia, and ultimately death. What is this... euthanasia?"

No sooner had I finished speaking, I realized what was happening. The doctors, who had given up on Mazen, were now giving him the license to die peacefully in his sleep rather than to endure the pain of acute headaches. If I was a doctor and knew the consequences of metastasized tumors, I too might have opted to give Mazen morphine as opposed to taking a chance on detracting from his dignity and allowing him to die in a vegetative state, but I wasn't a doctor and Mazen was my son, not my patient. Being agreeable to reason was a poor proposition.

Giving up? This is it? No way! This isn't going to happen.

I left the room, ran down the hall, and screamed for help. "I want my son's surgeon and I want him now!" I became louder and louder as I reached for the telephone behind the nurse's station. I was swept into the center of madness. I remembered Shirley MacLaine in *Terms of Endearment,* whose character's actions I thought exaggerated as she ran around the nurse's station screaming for someone to help her dying daughter, but as I was experiencing a matching hysteria, I thought…*she could have done more…*

No mother should have to watch her child go through what I label legalized euthanasia. The doctors were deliberately intervening in Mazen's life with the express intent of ending it to relieve his intractable suffering. Jack Kevorkian had been convicted of second-degree murder and served eight years because he had used a device called the "the Death Machine" or the gas mask that he called the "Mercy Machine" to painlessly end the lives of his patients. Many may disagree with me since it was the patient's choice, but I found it horrifying to watch some of his televised murders. I couldn't help but think that something parallel was happening to my son. True, Mazen was treated with morphine to appease his chronic pain, but he was physically healthy. If there were a miracle pill to treat his tumor, he would have taken it and resumed his normal life. Morphine should be used *only* when there is absolutely no *hope,* or when patients have lost their ability to function and live normal lives. This was not the case with Mazen. I was determined to take my chances. I screamed again for his surgeon. While waiting, I hammered away at the phone's keypad and dialed our uncle Robert's number.

"Hello," he said.

"They are killing Mazen. They're injecting him with morphine to ease his pain, but essentially, they are killing him. I refuse to watch him die this way. I want them to perform surgery!"

"No, no. Listen to me…surgery is dangerous. You may lose him during surgery. The tumor is sitting on the left side of his frontal lobe. If they go too deep, they may alter his personality functions. There is also a chance that he will die. Are you sure you want to do this?"

"Yes, I am positive. They are killing him anyway. Euthanasia is not an option even though his doctors wanted to be merciful. I spoke with Mona and she's on her way."

The nurses must have advised the surgeon of my behavior and he came running from the elevators. He stood next to me. He could hardly control his expression.

"Good enough," Robert said . "Is the surgeon nearby?"

"Yes, he just arrived. I'll give him the receiver."

After a lengthy discussion, the surgeon decided to perform surgery. When Mona arrived, the surgical team met with us and explained what the operation entailed, and discussed the possibility of treating Mazen with immunotherapy after his surgery. Immunotherapy would treat his disease by inducing, enhancing, or suppressing an immune response. He explained that a brain tumor never metastasizes, but if malignant, it will spread within the cranium and result in death. A careful study of Mazen's MRI revealed that his tumor infiltrated crucial areas of his brain with tiny fingers of malignant cells. This made it almost impossible to remove, but left it amenable to injections with healthy cells extracted from his body. These cells would be mixed with a chemical called Interleukin 2 and would work together to shrink the tumor.

Mona and I explained that we would research immunotherapy clinical studies and discuss our thoughts with him once Mazen recovered from surgery. The nurse approached us with a stack of papers. Mona signed them to surrender her rights to sue if Mazen died during surgery or became cognitively impaired. For all we knew and hoped, Mazen might not have a tumor at all. The nurses rushed him to the surgical unit. Mona and I followed.

I began to wonder whether surgery was a sound decision. If the surgeon went too deep, Mazen might die of blood loss or worse; if surgery destroyed too much healthy brain tissue, he might be better off without treatment. I hoped the surgeon would find no tumor and that, if he did, he would suction as much of it as possible to avoid hemorrhage and so to keep Mazen alive with little if any brain damage. Even though the doctor had explained that the operation was not violently dangerous and that they were simply going to extract an alien mass, I was still worried.

Once inside the surgical unit, I was told to wait in the family waiting room. Mona joined Mazen to hold his hand until they were ready to start the procedure. Forty-five minutes later, she came out screaming, "He's gone. He's gone! Mazen's dead. I don't know what's happening. He had severe tremors and jerking of the body. I don't know what they're doing to him. They told me to leave."

"No, Mona. Go back! Make sure he's not having more seizures. Please go back!"

I fell to my knees and prayed that Mazen was still alive and that God would give us more time with him. Ten minutes later, Mona returned. Her panicky face was replaced with a shadow of light and the hope he would survive the surgery.

"He's alive. They took him to surgery." She started crying.

Nine long hours had passed before a nurse came out and said, "Mazen is fine. The doctor will be out shortly to speak with you."

Close relatives and friends packed the family waiting room. Most everyone seemed tired and desperate for a word of encouragement.

The surgeon finally walked slowly into the room, approached Mona and me and said, "Can I speak with you in the consultation room?"

We trotted behind him.

Stillness fell upon me as I looked at his face. He looked like a corpse climbing out of its tomb. After standing for nine hours throughout Mazen's surgery, he appeared to have aged ten years. I was sick with fright and desperately waiting in what felt like the longest minute of my life. I broke the silence.

"Doctor, did you find a tumor?"

"Yes, there was a tumor and I was able to remove 25 percent of it, leaving vital areas of the brain with minimal injury. Mazen's tumor was like roots of a plant spread through soil. The surgery was challenging and that's why it took nine hours. We used innovative techniques to optimize the surgical debulking of his tumor. One thing I know is that it will reduce the pressure around his brain and relieve his symptoms. For the moment, he is fine. He will be under close observation until tomorrow and should be ready to go home in about a week. With your consent, I hope to start him on immunotherapy in two weeks. It has proven to reduce, sometimes eliminate, the tumors in over 85 percent of my patients. Believe me; they are much older than Mazen. If you'd like to learn more about immunotherapy, please stop by my office early next week to pick some literature. I believe it is covered under his insurance."

Beaten by the pressure of the day, he walked away with a pale face, having used up a considerable amount of his mental resources. He left us to celebrate the semi-success of Mazen's surgery.

Chapter 9

Suspended Hope

Following surgery, immediately upon opening his eyes, Mazen looked at me with his radiant smile and moved his lips as if to say, "Hi, Mom."

"Hey... Mazen," I said with a smile. "Are your headaches gone?" I had hoped his smile was a sign of relief. He nodded to indicate *yes*. I squeezed his hand, and said, "Thank God!"

But his comfort did not stop me from raising questions in my mind with each answer ending in another question. I didn't feel relieved since more than half the tumor was still there. I feared if his cancer took a swift, monstrous turn, creating voracious growth that would ultimately damage the remaining healthy tissue in his brain, my battle would be over.

I looked at him once more, trying to dismiss the blurry images of his future, and noticed that his eyes were no longer coordinated. The left eye had a slight droop, making his large and black eyes somewhat less engaging and more somber. His swollen face and shaved head made me wonder, if once alert, he would show signs of memory loss. Again, I reminded myself to think positive.

With disease and treatment, there is often suffering and discomfort. To my relief, Mazen made a quick recovery. The first thing he said was, "When can I go home? I miss the kids."

I looked at Mona and smiled. "That's the Mazen I know."

I placed my fears to rest.

Mazen was a passionate father. His children hovered around him like bees to honey. I thought of the day he was first diagnosed and when he'd arrived home from the hospital. His first inclination was to run to his children's bedrooms to make sure they were covered and sound asleep. Mona and I followed because he'd gone up the stairs in such haste that we thought something was wrong with him. As I watched him embrace his children and run his hand across their foreheads, I prayed that he would overcome his illness, wiped away my tears, and left for the evening.

The results of his surgery gave me reason to believe that there might be *hope* after all. I looked at him with an escalating mood, "Oh, the children are fine and you should be able to go home in about a week. His doctor said that the surgery went well."

He beamed. The breath of life fashioned itself around his positive spirit. "Sounds good . . . Maybe I can go back to work. What do you think?"

"Maybe..." I said, trying not to tell him that more than half the tumor was still growing in his head. I left the room.

Prior to his surgery and immediately following his diagnosis, he returned to work but was reluctant to tell his coworkers and employer that he was seriously ill. A business major, he worked in sales for F D Products Company, categorized under wholesale restaurant equipment and supplies. Frank D. Stella, the company's founder and owner, was a man to whom I will always extend the utmost admiration even though he is no longer among us. Frank had sensed that something was wrong with Mazen and invited him to his office. Mazen broke out in tears as he shared the results of his diagnosis with him. Frank held Mazen's hand and said, "Go home and don't worry about a thing. I want you to take good care of yourself and come back when you're ready. You are ambitious, but your health comes first. Your character, business spirit, and commitment to recruiting new clients have made a positive contribution to the company's success. You have nothing to worry about. I will keep you on the company's insurance policy, and I will continue to send you a paycheck. Just keep me updated."

Mazen was speechless as Frank walked him to his car and gave him a tight hug. When Mazen shared what had happened with me, I noted how God was already making me feel better about a situation that was so devastating and dreadful.

After surgery, Mazen resumed a normal home life but never returned to work. Surgery had caused minimal short-term memory loss, making it difficult for him to drive and remember routes. Somewhat apprehensive, Mona and I researched immunotherapy and found that clinical trials resulted in improved clinical outcomes and that the sooner Mazen started the better.

He started immunotherapy two weeks after surgery. The treatment caused spectacular improvement. I wasn't sure whether his recovery was due to the surgery, immunotherapy, his youth and growth of healthy cells, the human spirit, or a combination of all these. It really didn't matter. He was walking, playing with his children, participating in family outings and picnics, and most of all, he was happy. Unaware where all the happiness was going to lead, I was thrilled as I watched him find comfort in exercising his role as a father.

I continued to shield Mazen from a certain, obvious knowledge. He had a strong will to live, if not for himself, for the sake of his wife and children. He might have been aware of what was going on, but rarely did he allow the bottom layer of his consciousness to surface. At times, I knew he was worried when he'd stare out his living room window, lower his chin, and take deep, long-lasting breaths. It wasn't until months later while chatting with him at his home that he spoke to me about his fears. We were sitting across from each other in his cozy living room. He was listening to soft, instrumental Lebanese music without lyrics, and I was writing my daily journal on my laptop.

He looked at me and said, "Mom, will you write a letter to my wife and give it to her at the right time?"

I didn't know what the right time was, and I didn't want to ask. I could only think…he was too young to open his heart to death. He knew all along the seriousness of his illness, but he preferred not to talk about it.

I stood up and in a casual tone said, "Mazen, hold on to your dreams and listen to the rhythm of your heart. Don't let fragments of your life be washed away by the stillness of the night. Without *hope*, where would your power be? You need to open to your inner knowledge and healing. You are going to be fine."

Friends and family visited with him, each expressing interest in taking him to ball games, the movies, or outings that did not require a modicum of guidance or assistance. Color, light, joy, and laughter were embedded in his relationship with his children. I watched as they danced around him, sang to him, jumped over his back and shoulders, and smothered his face with butterfly kisses. He treated each of them in a special way. They were exciting and pleasant variations of each other, and their laughter traveled across the room with a glowing radiance and a sense of ripeness.

Unfortunately, six months after his surgery, a dark shadow settled in his home to remind us of the seriousness of his illness. Mazen began to experience weakness in the right arm and right leg. He had difficulty walking steadily or standing in the same spot. After he fell several times in one day, we contacted his neurologist. He implored us with the utmost urgency to start radiation.

The radiologist recommended focused radiation therapy, a therapy that aimed directly at the tumor and its immediate surrounding area. I would have preferred Gamma Knife, a radio-surgery that is not really surgery, but it was only available in California at the time. It delivered a pinpoint dose of radiation from hundreds of angles. It sounded like a better option, but the doctors did not believe that Mazen was physically fit to travel.

My cousin Helal, a radiology specialist and good friend of Mazen's was assigned to administer his radiation. Mazen and I walked into the room where the radiation was to be performed. Mona decided to wait alone.

Helal took me to the side and while holding back his tears, whispered, "I'm having a very hard time with this, but I will do my best to make him comfortable." He walked over to Mazen and jokingly said, "Hey, Mazen, luckily you're lying down and you don't have to bear the weight of this metal helmet. It's not just any helmet. It has hundreds of holes in it."

Mazen feigned a smile and turned his head away. Helal exhaled. In a more formal tone he said, "I am going to target the beams of radiation directly at the tumor to avoid damage to healthy tissue. It is a local therapy, and it will only affect the cells in its path. This may only take a few minutes. Trust me. You won't feel a thing. I will repeat the process once a day for the next five days and then your doctor will probably send you home."

Mona was sitting still in the corner of the room adjacent to the x-ray room. She was struggling with further trials and doubts. Fear of the unknown had taken its sad toll on her, and the last thing she wanted was to suspend her hope. I wanted to comfort her, but I too was afraid of the mutations of Mazen's tumor. Nothing I said would have made a difference.

Mona was a stay-at-home mom. She worried about her husband, her future, and the future of her children. She showed signs of restlessness throughout the day and I'd catch her gasping for breath frequently.

Observing her at that moment, I wanted to say, *I know what you are thinking and I know how hard it may be for you to imagine that something could ever happen to Mazen, but we both believe there is a high probability that some volcanic force might reduce his brain tumor, and sustain our hope. If I could trade my life for his, I would have done so in a second. Do you think I would care for life if Mazen's is gone? I don't think so. But life can be cruel and losing my husband, the father of my children, was devastating. I couldn't make sense of his death, but life pulled me along whether I blessed it or not. I discovered that there is no rationality to death. The conflict of living alone through the struggles of life can be cruel and painful.*

In the midst of my struggles, my mother once said to me, "Are you crying because your husband died and you have to work? You better pull yourself together, get out there, and do what you need to do to support your family. I have yet to see anyone die from work."

I had expected a hug, not a lecture. But I learned at that moment that feeling sorry for myself wasn't an option. On the contrary, I became stronger and more determined to move forward. *Mona*, I thought, *I pray day and night that Mazen remains among us, but at the same time, you need to get ready for the worst.* I knew from the averted faces of his doctors that he would probably die, but I refused to surrender my motherhood.

Instead of voicing my thoughts, I sat next to her and said, "Mona, you went to school to become a teacher and you taught adult education, so I know you have experience. How about if you start working? I have many friends in the school system, and if you get hired, you'll get a break from the daily pressure you are experiencing and you'll have a secure income in case Frank stops sending Mazen a paycheck. I can switch my schedule to afternoons to be with Mazen and baby Jemail in the morning. Then perhaps Rania, Dania, Ernie, or my niece, Jenny, can take turns to be with them in the afternoon. Keep in mind that I will always extend a helping hand, but eventually, you will need to be physically and financially independent. What do you think?"

"I don't know. I'll think about it," she said and started to weep.

Chapter 10

Magnetic Fields

I became a regular at the hospital's imaging center. Mazen's doctors were constantly requesting MRIs and other brain scans to measure the growth or reduction in the size of his tumor as they planned for future treatments. I decided to stop weeping behind closed doors, overcome my feelings, and participate in the planning. I was prepared to get into the soul of what medicine had to offer, but I wasn't sure whether the doctors would be willing to surrender to my suggestions.

One morning soon after we'd arrived at the radiology department, the nurse walked into the waiting room and asked Mazen to follow her. It was about 5:45 a.m. The hospital was deserted. There was no sound except for the hollow echo of warm air seeping through the dusty vents. While waiting, I watched the nurse through the transparent glass prepare Mazen for the MRI procedure. Once ready, she waved at the imaging technologist to start.

Cold and restless, I walked over to the technologist and said, "Can I sit next to you?"

"Sure," he replied, still focused on the computer screen.

"It's cold down here, isn't it?" I said, wondering if he even heard me.

A few minutes later, he turned around. "Are you his mother?"

"Yes, yes, I am," I said with a firm tone, wondering why he wanted to know.

The nurse had given Mazen a small dose of valium to help keep him immobile within the large powerful magnet, while the technologist used magnetic fields and radio waves to produce high-quality two- and three-dimensional images of his brain structures without use of x-rays or radioactive tracers. I observed the images of Mazen's tumor across the screen and tried to decipher them. The observations felt like pins puncturing at my temples, but I continued to analyze the internal structures of his brain. I was looking at cross-sectional slices from many angles, as if looking at a slice of his brain from the front, from the side, or from above his head.

I armored my teary eyes with iron panes and balanced judgment. I knew that it wasn't time to cry, but time to forge strength out of weakness, and time for *hope* to direct the course of my thinking.

With Mazen on one side of the glass and me on the other, I did not know that my fascination with the human brain, learning, memory, and retention during my postgraduate years would lead me to study the images and functions of my son's brain in the face of stress that at times, mobilized my thought processes. I had studied images of functional MRIs to observe changes in blood flow and brain activity to understand whole brain learning, but this was totally different. The images I saw in front of me were actual pictures of Mazen's tumor, showing the lesion as a bright area of high-signal intensity in the left hemisphere of his brain.

I smiled and looked at the technologist. "They look the same as the images his doctors had shared with me last week. His tumor has not grown. Maybe the treatment is working and his condition is stabilizing. I can't wait to see his doctors."

Although the technician ignored my observations and continued to take pictures, he seemed caring and understanding. I learned later that he was married to Mona's cousin and that Mazen was no stranger to him.

The next day, Mazen's doctors discussed his condition with me and agreed that it had stabilized, but they weren't sure to which extent and whether the tumor might still grow and damage eloquent areas of his brain. I suggested targeted drug therapy.

Targeted drug treatments concentrate on precise abnormalities present within cancer cells. By blocking these abnormalities, targeted drug treatments can cause cancer cells to die. One physician looked at me and said, "We can talk about alternative treatments at length once I rule out all other options."

I feared the spread of abnormal brain cells and wondered how long anyone could live with them? My fears continued to grow stronger with time.

The brain, a complex organ that allows us to think, smell, see, taste, hear, move, and feel became the system that dominated my thoughts and influenced my thinking during the span of Mazen's illness. I was frustrated. I didn't know enough about tumors and neurology. I wanted to learn more.

I explained my desire and purpose to the Dean of Admissions at one of the local medical schools. I asked him for permission to take a few medical school courses on brain anatomy and neurology. I had hoped that by doing so, I would expand my knowledge of brain tumors, their symptoms, causes, and treatments. The Dean explained that the courses were about neuroscience in general and not brain-tumor specific. He also explained that they might be quite challenging and that he would only allow me to audit the courses. I accepted, and during the fall of 1999, I spent my evenings at Wayne State University to study neuroscience.

I found that brain tumors are among the third leading cause of cancer deaths for young adults ages twenty to thirty-nine, but despite all of the research in the field, it was not clear what caused them. I wanted to find a reason. I wavered back and forth only to conclude that *reason* was withered away by *unreason*. Did living in war-torn Lebanon for ten years cause Mazen's tumor? Cancer arises from damage to cellular respiration. Respiratory damage is irreversible. Did he inhale chemical residues from shattered missiles and weaponries that exploded around our building during periods of heavy shelling? Each time a bomb fell to the ground, he'd run outside to observe the damage. I shared this information with his doctors, but not one of them would confirm or deny my extrapolation. By the end of the fall semester, I realized that a few courses were not going to turn me into a neurologist and that my only fallback was to associate with people who shared my experiences. I ached to find other inklings of *hope*.

The National Brain Tumor Foundation (NBTF) founded in 1981, offered support to patients and their families through the distribution of literature, brochures, and brain tumor conferences. In December of 1999, I registered to attend the March 2000 NBTF conference in Los Angeles. I outlined the sessions that I wanted to attend in advance and planned on meeting with neurologists and other experts in the field. I wanted to make sure that I knew about all brain tumor medical advances around the country.

By January of 2000, Mazen's tumor was showing signs of new growth and his doctors were seeing him less. He had difficulty walking steadily, and I dreaded what lay ahead. The radiation had relieved him for a while, but the right side of his body had become frail. We stood around him inconspicuously to prevent or to cushion a potential fall. Mazen complained of excruciating headaches one morning and we rushed him to emergency. The doctor looked at him and said, "If hydrocephalus is present, you may need a shunt to drain cerebrospinal fluid."

Mazen turned his face toward me inquisitively. The doctor noticed, looked him in the eye and stated, "A shunt is a long, thin tube placed in a ventricle of the brain and then threaded under the skin to another part of the body, usually the abdomen. It works like a drainpipe. Excess fluid is carried away from the brain and is absorbed in the abdomen, and in some cases, the fluid is drained into the heart."

My lips tightened as I whispered under my breath, *I hope Mazen's not one of those cases.* The area around his forehead had begun to swell. The surgeon inserted a shunt that reduced the swelling significantly.

Mazen also did physical and occupational therapy three times a week, but no sooner than he learned a new method to compensate for a permanently damaged skill than he'd get temporarily better at it, but worse in another. It was like building sand towers of hope near the ocean shore and watching winter tides devour them—one at a time.

Mazen lost his geographic concept of space after his brain tumor surgery and I feared allowing him out of my sight. He lost his free spirit and his flowery smile. If I were helping him work on one of his exercises, he'd say, "I really don't want to take up your time, Mom. I want to learn how to help myself. I want to get better on my own."

Listening to his words taught me the art of tender silence and the power of nonverbal communication. I'd smile and give him a warm hug. I felt like a flower yielding its nectar to a hungry bee. Mazen's emotions were genuine. His teary eyes spoke to me in abundance. He was soundlessly asking me to build him a house of affection and to soothe the pain of his bleeding wound. With very little to work with, I realized that I was running out of time in a world of tension and despair. Mazen was the source of my energy, the fragrance of my life, and the warmth of my soul. I wasn't ready to lose *hope*.

I phoned my best friend Wafa, who lived in Africa, and asked her to visit with me. I could not dispel the fear in my heart. I explained to her that Mazen's tests were showing tumor growth and that his doctors were losing hope. I needed to hear words of comfort. She was the kind of friend who took action and knew how to reach out. She never said, *Oh, I'm so sorry* or *I wish I could do something to relieve your stress*, but rather, listened patiently to my crying and called me on a daily basis to see how I was doing. She lived in Dakar, Senegal, thousands of miles across the ocean, but promised she'd come and visit once I returned from the brain tumor conference. I needed her beside me, at least for a short while. Mazen waved at me and said, "Mom, tell her to come. I'd like to see her too."

My son and I stood weak in the face of fear and the tumor's

ruthless assault. Nothing made sense to us anymore. Our emotions had crippled our hope and tangled the threads of our rational minds.

Emotional centers that neuroscientists have found in specific areas of the brain are fear and pleasure. Mazen was frustrated and tense each time he failed to perform a specific task or failed to learn a new way to compensate for a lost skill. He was too proud to accept failure and too weak to conquer the seat of his fear. He'd rather fall than to ask for help and he'd rather be silent than to beckon sympathy. Everything that made him the person that he was stemmed from within the membranes of his brain through processes so impressively interconnected that I could not fathom the thought that one day, something might cause his faculties or his senses to desert him entirely. I no longer took any of his skills or senses for granted, especially after his loss of muscle control.

One early afternoon, Mazen looked at me and in what sounded like a deep murmur said, "Mom, I can barely keep my eyes open and each time I say something, people ask me to repeat what I said. Should I remain silent? What is happening to me?"

Mazen, now handcuffed to the windows of darkness, felt helpless. I thought for a moment and looked him in the eye. "Well, you are working with a physical therapist. I'm sure he'll help build your strength back in no time." My white lies were traveling with the wind, and the hand of life was releasing itself from Mazen's grip. I wasn't ready to succumb to Mazen's fate. I had to make a shift.

I knew that the world of conventional medicine was failing him, but I was determined to continue with hope even though the rainbow of hope was creeping behind the arc of its reflection. I wanted him to stay strong and cling to life like a delicate butterfly hatching out of its pupa.

By March of 2000, my husband and I were preparing for the NBTF conference. I called my brother Jamal, who lived in Oakland, California at the time, to inform him of my decision to go to the NBTF.

His wife Amina took the phone from him in delight. "I'm so

glad you're coming to California. I want to tell you about a woman who lives in Mexico. She has been a lifesaver for many people. One of my Spanish friends suggested that Mazen visit with a *curandera*, a "woman healer" from Mexicali, Mexico, whose prayers helped to heal the terminally ill. My friend told me that her mother had been diagnosed with terminal cancer and had been given less than a year to live. Guess what? It's been five years and she's doing great! You know what? I want to go see her too. My migraines are unbearable. Maybe she can help me."

I froze for a moment thinking...*does science mean anything after all? How can this be true?* Startled and excited by her suggestion, I said, "Amina, please tell me more about this woman. Is she really a healer? Does she use herbal medicine? How long will it take to see her? Do we have to set up an appointment? Can I see her immediately after the conference? Does Mazen have to be with me? Does she have a healing touch? You are giving me hope when hope has been slipping away for weeks."

Unprepared to answer my questions, she called me back the following morning and said, "If Mazen cannot come, you will need to bring a shirt that he has worn for a few days so that the healer can connect with his scent. She will see us without an appointment, but it'll take about eight hours of driving from my home to her residence in Mexico. I have all the information we need. Call me when you're done with the conference. We'll pick you up and drive down to Mexico."

Amina gave me a string of hope that reached beyond the reality of medicinal cure. She was a pharmacist, yet medicine was failing her, and she'd hoped to find a spiritual cure for her health problems. The uveal tract behind her eyes was inflamed, and she was experiencing severe migraines and problems with her vision. She was born and raised in Venezuela, so I knew Spanish was not going to be a barrier. She would serve as my translator.

I flew to Los Angeles, California, on, Thursday, March 30, 2000, with my husband Ernie and our two-year-old son, Adam.

Chapter 11

Twisted Triangle of Faith

The NBTF conference was scheduled for Friday, March 31, but I'd planned to arrive a day early to be rested and well prepared for a weekend of talks and interactions. I was eager to learn more about cancer biology, genetics, stem cell studies, and the rebooting of the immune system. Mazen's tumor had been growing rapidly, and I was in search of a treatment that would kill tumor cells while minimizing toxicity to the adjoining healthy tissues of his brain. Because Mazen was already doing immunotherapy, I was interested in the immune system. I wanted to know how well the human body was prepared to locate, attack, and eliminate cancerous cells. I stopped by Mazen's house on my way to the airport to hug him and to take one of his shirts with me. Bedridden, sightless, and inarticulate, the warmth of his hand transmitted waves of selfless love that landed in my heart to help me walk the path of hope anew. For what he suffered, he never uttered a word of blasphemy or signaled a sign of irreverence toward God. His submissiveness was unique.

Speechless, I thought of Mazen's spirit, as he lay withdrawn, his fallen eyelids and his slack limbs creating re-energized passion to travel through my body. After feeling the soft touch of his cheek against my lips as I kissed him good-bye, the pillar of my faith rose ten-fold. God is not asleep. He is watching over you, and He will hear your cry for mercy. I squeezed his hand tightly. "I promise to do my best. I pray the medical field will suggest new treatments and drugs that will improve your situation. I took your shirt so that I can give it to the Mexican *curandera*. Maybe she can connect with your scent and make you feel better before I even come back. I love you. I'll be back in about a week."

Once on board the plane, I fell silently into despair, fearing the unknown. I took a deep breath, and prepared for takeoff.

The flight attendant walked down the aisle to make sure that all seat belts were fastened. Throughout the five-hour journey to Los Angeles, I took the challenge of outsmarting her by camouflaging the belt fastener with my hand each time the plane shook from turbulence and the seat belt signal lit up. I didn't think that she'd understand or give me a gentle smile if I told her that I no longer feared the bitterness of death. After Mazen's diagnosis, death came barging through the corridors of my consciousness and I'd become accustomed to listening to its omnipotent tune from sunrise to sunset. I frequently thought that if Mazen were to die, I wanted to die with him. Parents shouldn't have to run against the course of nature and outlive their children, and if death were inevitable, maybe stoicism should become a worldwide practice.

Fully alert, I was prepared to conduct a lengthy conversation with my husband and review the summaries of the brain tumor sessions we were going to attend, but baby Adam was sleeping quietly in his arms and I dared not speak. I looked away, drifting into the angles and bends of the rushing aircraft as it soared along the misty paths of the cosmos between Detroit and LA.

As it became dark, even though we were instructed to pull the window shades down, I left mine open. I wanted to occupy my mind with the ancient tales of the constellations, myths that told the tales of gods and heroes and how mysterious forces of the universe gave answers to the wonders of life and death. It was time out of the present, a time when the vibrations of the plane's engine felt like a good omen. The mid- and high-frequency sounds that emanated from the jet engines didn't bother me. Rather, they lifted my spirits as though a generous gift from God, who at that time, had arranged to sweep away my grief and melancholic sorrows. I sensed Him whispering directly into my ears, *you can't afford to be apprehensive; you need to focus.*

The following morning after breakfast, we left Adam with a group of babysitter volunteers on the second floor directly above the conference rooms and went to our first session on cancer biology and genetics. The researcher had investigated the cellular and genetic abnormalities that drive the biology of brain tumors. He revealed that he and his team had uncovered clues to which genetic factors were involved in tumor development and found that stem cells play a role in certain brain tumors.

I sat in the front row to listen attentively and to take notes, but it was difficult to write and process information simultaneously. *I should have brought a tape recorder. . .*I thought as I continued to jot notes. I wanted to savor the trail of his words, as heady to me as incense; that is, until I found myself lost. His words were lucid, but the concept behind them was difficult to digest. The words had an unconventional beat that scrambled my connection with reality. I could no longer separate the positive from the negative effects of what turned into a dragging moment. The session became heavy and dark, more theoretical and utterly different from the sweet, thin aroma of Mazen's doctors' informed impressions in Detroit. When all else seemed to be failing, His doctors' theories usually lulled me into a rush of hope against the shallow banks of despair.

I took comfort in congregating with physicians and speakers as I walked in and out of sessions to listen to new ideas and theories. My goal was to improve Mazen's life, not enclose him in a triangle of hope, scientific experimentation, and frustration. As much as the sessions brought together stimulating interaction, discussions, and aspirations to patients whose cancer was still in its early phases, this was not the case for Mazen. I had longed for a drug or treatment that might suspend his tumor growth, but instead, I felt disappointed, maybe even deceived. I found that despite years of experimentations and massive amounts of resources funneled into cancer research, approximately 90 percent of potential oncology drugs failed in late-stage clinical trials. The complex intricacy of each individual's cancer, the clinical trials, and what I call the cancer cells' *centralized energy,* were factored in as a reason for the high rate of disappointments.

Brain tumors are complex and as a result, dynamic approaches are usually required to combat such a deadly disease. Most of what I heard was based on research methods that were not noteworthy. I wasn't willing to embrace leading-edge pharmaceuticals that might cause Mazen more harm than good. His body was too weak, and, unless doctors and researchers were able to predict with a fair amount of accuracy how Mazen's individual tumor was going to react to potential drug therapies, I was not going to take a chance. I feared that many of the cancer cells had already slipped away from the brain and were causing damage somewhere else. I had hope that immunotherapy would elicit an immune response for at least three, maybe even five years, but instead, Mazen's tumor continued to grow. I walked away from the morning sessions feeling dolorous and heavy-hearted. Nothing was automatic. I'd hoped the sessions would make me feel better and release the pressure of my malaise, but instead, it was like sacrificing a newborn to the Temple of Baal. *Was there really a cure, or was I contending with the inevitable?*

I was too beat to climb the flight of stairs, so I took the elevator to the second floor to check on Adam. I held his little body securely against my bosom, took Ernie's hand. "Please take charge of him. I'm going to skip lunch and pick up a few brochures from the kiosks in the main lobby."

"Not a problem. I'll be at the restaurant downstairs if you feel like joining me for coffee when you're done."

Back in the lobby, I heard music flowing from around the corner. *Who could be playing music at a brain tumor conference?* I followed the sound to enter a room swollen with listeners and stood transfixed by what I was hearing. The music and lyrics of the young singer tore me away from darkness. My nerves tingled from the warmth of his words and my heart was guided by the tenderness of his fluctuating musical notes. It was the artist and singer, David M. Bailey. He had been diagnosed four years earlier with a glioblastoma multiforme (GBM), usually a fatal form of brain cancer, and to the puzzlement of his caring physicians, he survived with his tumor years beyond their predictions. David inspired me to defy terminal diagnostic reports. He was a gifted singer, songwriter, and guitarist who lived to prove his physicians wrong. He appeared healthy and buoyant as I listened to him sing *"One More Day."*

Doctors whom David labeled "cynics" are not always right. I renounced my desire to drink from the silver cup of tests and theories and embraced his belief in drinking from the fountain of hope. I thought he was magnificent—aloof in a kingdom of his own. The lines between conventional and alternative medicine became so blurred that I decided to investigate further the natural healing process. I wondered if David's words were a legitimate response to mainstream medicine's real shortcomings. I yearned to join his world.

Chapter 12

La Curandera

I wish I could have walked away from the conference carrying a torch of triumph, but instead, I felt like a wounded warrior searching for refuge on yet another battlefield. I never left a conference so confused and disappointed. I was disappointed, not with the programs or speakers, but with the solid fact that there was no hope for Mazen to recover. Not even to improve. I felt coerced into letting go of the presumption that science would produce any sort of positive outcome and gave way to the wonders of supernatural healing.

I knew at that point that I had to forsake conventional treatments and exchange the executioner dwelling in my head for a restorer of faith and positive expectations. Nothing from the world of scholarly guidance gave me hope. I couldn't stop thinking about David M. Bailey's fortune and optimism. I looked at my husband on the final evening of the conference as we walked into our hotel room and said, "I'm ready for Mexicali."

I couldn't wait to see the *curandera*.

The next morning, we packed our belongings and waited for

my brother Jamal and his wife Amina to pick us up. I sat on my suitcase, scattered Adam's toys around a small piece of carpet near the coffee table in the corner of the front lobby and watched him run his airplane across the floor. His tiny lips simulated the blast of engines while his arms soared over the sofa that his father was sitting on and around to the outer edge of my suitcase. It reminded me of Mazen and how even though thirty years had passed, a young life can be cut short in a heartbeat. I reminisced over the fortune-tellers of my past. I wondered how they differed from the *curandera* whom I had become very anxious to meet.

When I lived in Africa I'd visited with fortune-tellers and listened attentively to their predictions, but I will always remember the Frenchman who was the last to read my fortune before I permanently left Africa. He lived on the eleventh floor of a high rise in Dakar, Senegal. He foretold the future using a deck of cards with full-tone colors. They were accentuated with jumbo numbers, letters, and emotion-evoking images. I had decided to see him after I'd read in the paper that the president of Senegal, Leopold Sedar Senghor, and his wife were stimulated by what this Frenchman had told them, and they had visited him more than once. My sister-in-law, Zahira, who was usually my fortune-teller companion, had some reservations before she followed me into the elevator. She yanked my arm and said, "What if he's psychopathic and does something to harm us? He can do a lot of things in half an hour."

"Don't worry. If we don't like what we see when he opens the door, we'll run back to the elevator. Just hold the door open, silly..."

As soon as he opened the door and I saw his amiable face covered with a coat of light foundation and his puffy lips painted with bright, red lipstick, I smiled. I looked at Zahira, and said, "Wait for me in the lobby. I'll be down in thirty minutes."

"Are you sure I can leave you alone?"

"Yes, I'm sure. Can't you see? He's gay... He looks like he is very personable and caring."

The psychic's knowledge of my past was legit and his predictions of my future materialized four months later. He told me that my family and I were going to permanently leave Africa and live in a country torn by war. He told me that I was going through some rough times on a personal level, but that I was going to find comfort in my new home. Even though the Quran condemns fortune-tellers, he told me the truth, yet I didn't want to associate him with the *curandera* because I didn't want to do anything to upset God.

So I convinced myself that *curandera* means "to heal" and fortune-teller means "to predict." I wondered... *was there a difference or perhaps a balance between the two? Does either of them have the power to connect with God? Was la curandera a saint? Did she have a special relationship with God? What about the medical community? Is there anything scientific about curanderas that might give patients hope? Would it be religiously acceptable if she were a scientist? Was she someone I could trust?*

Thinking about all these questions confused me again. Lost in my thoughts, I reflected upon what one of my science professors had told the class while I was at the University of Senegal in the '70s. He described how his brother, who ran a psychiatry clinic in Diourbel, a small village in Senegal, found that, after a few weeks of treatment, many of his schizophrenic patients left his clinic to seek the help of the "Medicine Man." Puzzled, he followed one of his patients, whose family members had snatched him away from the clinic in the middle of the night.

He parked his car at the outskirts of the village and tried to stay out of sight. He observed his patient roll in circles on the sandy ground. The patient grumbled and moaned as though he were in pain. The inhabitants of the village stood close by to cheer him on. The medicine man stood across from him spreading his powers through ritual dancing, charms, and chants. After two hours of non-conventional treatment, the young man stood up and walked away with a great sense of normality. He was content and so was his family. The doctor later learned that the medicine man had the most revered body of healing knowledge next to the chief of the village and had received his powers through training and a special diet. I couldn't help but think...*Does this mean that there's still hope for Mazen? Do ordinary people have healing powers? I hope so...*

The *curandera* we were going to see was Catholic. Catholics are very dear to Muslims and the Quran affirms that all monotheistic religions shall have their reward from God. Islam emphasizes the importance of prayer and how if you ask God for help, He will assist you. Since much of *curanderismo,* the art of healing, involves prayer, then the woman healer whom I planned to visit would most certainly help Mazen through the power of her prayer. Based on what Amina knew, the *curandera* had helped many whose conditions were determined to be fatal to live a normal life through her prayers.

Amina, who learned about *curanderas* through her Catholic mother, told me that a true *curandera,* or *curandera total,* possesses the divine gift of healing. She needs only her head, her hands, and her heart to reach out to the body and the soul. She should be capable of developing an individualized curing method for her visitors. The *curandera* whom we were going to see preferred to stay at her home in front of her own sacred altars. Amina had informed me that the *curandera* used water to draw away negative energy and herb tea to heal the soul. Amina stressed that it was important for me to believe in the operative elements of healing before embarking on our journey.

The ringing of the phone broke my reverie in the lobby.

"Hey, Sis. We're on our way. We prepared sandwiches, filled the cooler with soft drinks, fruits, and vegetables and brought many snacks. It's an eight-hour journey and between your restless son and my demanding two daughters, it is going to be a long ride. But on the bright side, I informed the *curandera* of our visit and she's waiting for us."

"Great! I look forward to seeing her...I mean you and your family."

Chapter 13

The Black Curse

My desperation had turned into fear, and it became evident that there was a clear divide between my feelings and my reactions to those feelings. Just when I thought I had everything under control, my empire of hope fell into darkness. I could no longer measure a cure by time in the near or distant future. I could only measure it by what is—and the "is" was the present. I was forced to live with the obvious—Mazen's condition was deteriorating and the conference had merely served as a platform for writers and publishers. There were no answers to be found there. The *curandera* was my last sliver of hope. I couldn't wait for Jamal and Amina to arrive.

Once settled in our car for the eight-hour trip, I was confident we were on our way to meet with the neutralizer of all things past. I didn't know what to say, or how to thank my closest family members, or even my husband, who from time to time reached out to massage my neck and draw me closer to him. Everyone was silenced by my sniffles—even the children, as I wept and spoke of my frustration with the conference and my dismantled hope. I don't know if children understand why adults cry, but it seemed that when I did, their innocent faces resembled wilted flowers. I took control of my emotions and stopped crying even though I didn't want to be bothered with the burden of where and when to cry. I ached to express my gratitude to Jamal, Amina, and Ernie for their devotion and passion in joining me on my journey. I was afraid that if I said anything, they'd feel offended. They made it clear that they wanted to help. They too, were looking for a cure not yet voiced.

I couldn't control my emotions. My thoughts turned into sobs. I swallowed the drainage running down my throat and watched my tears fall into my lap. Amina turned around, reached over her seat, touched my hand, and said, "Please don't cry. We're getting closer to the truth. We need to place our hope in silent healing and divine energy."

The drive down Interstate 5 was more a time to seek diversion, or an intermission to allow the full measure of reality declare itself, than an opportunity to contemplate creation and the good in people. Jamal must have sensed that I was feeling guilty for taking up his time and for asking him to take me to see the *curandera*, because he wanted to put my mind at ease. He turned his head sideways and said, "Listen, I know you're hurting, but so am I. I am hurting for you, and I'm hurting for Mazen. Don't think for a second that I am doing this just for you. I love Mazen and I would do anything to find him a cure, and I don't want you to think at any point that you're making me do something I don't want to do."

Hesitant to say thank you, I still reached over and patted him on the shoulder. "I love you." I knew he was telling the truth. Mazen had a strong bond with all of my brothers. After his father died, he depended upon my brother Jamal's compassion, my brother Sammy's high-tech and mechanical guidance, and my brother Joe's sagacity and business skills. They treated him as their own son and Mazen respected them for that. He followed them to Philadelphia to work with them in the pizza businesses. He was caring of their wives and children and spent his early twenties painting his world around the concept that altruism should be lived and nurtured and that family was of the essence. Mazen visited more with my brothers than he did his friends. He carried their children in his arms as if he were their father and embraced their family culture.

My husband too, learned to love and appreciate Mazen over the eight-year period that he had known him. He admired Mazen for his maturity and pleasant personality. Mazen stood each time he saw Ernie to shake his hand or to embrace him. He spoke to him about life, politics, and religion. Mazen gave the impression that he was years older than his biological age and once immersed in conversation with him, his stories resonated with an intensified sense of subjective dimension.

Mazen respected everyone. He respected the young, the old, all races, all ethnicities. He respected cultural diversity, and peoples' choices. Seven years after the death of his father, he respected my choice of Ernie in marriage and embraced me with a firm hug when he learned that I was pregnant with Adam a few years later. Moreover, when I'd told him that I was self-conscious of my pregnancy because I was forty-six at the time, he said, "You're just bringing another lucky person into this world. There's nothing to be self-conscious about."

There was a sort of true harmony between Mazen and me that passed to my husband and led him to factor the *curandera* into his engineering mindset and find room for spiritual knowledge and healing. Ernie realized that scientific thinking was something that was social in nature and not an innate manifestation inside peoples' heads. As much as his silence played a negative role in my hopes for a cure through non-conventional medicine, a few weeks prior to our trip, he too became married to my belief.

I spent most of the drive speaking to him slowly about specific treatments and herbs that might treat Mazen's physical symptoms and the spiritual components of his illness. I affixed a scientific tag to each of the success stories that I had shared with him only to retain my own sanity and belief that in the event I was wrong, I could always revert to scientific theory.

Ernie poked my arm and shook me out of my trance, "Hey, we're here."

I straightened my posture and sat alert to my surroundings. The US border at Tijuana was crowded and chaotic. I'm not sure what my sister-in-law told the border patrol, but they instantly waved us through. "Buena suerte," they said.

Amina had the *curandera's* address written on a small piece of paper. She ran her fingers across a map she must have downloaded off the internet to navigate Jamal through town and lead him to Mexicali. The children were wide-awake and fussy. We stopped at McDonald's in Tijuana's *Zona Centro* for a restroom break, coffee, and ice cream before continuing to Mexicali. I was amazed at how McDonald's rented its rooftops to business owners to display their ads on billboards alongside the restaurant chain's big yellow and red sign. Once inside, I could not take my eyes off the vivid hangings covering the walls, with rigid patterns that were both delicate and bold. I wondered if this was a formal greeting or glimpse into where I was heading. We bumped into people as we climbed up to the second floor where there seemed to be more room for the children to run around. The sun was low. The wind was crying from heat. Instead of coffee, we ordered lemonade and fell into a trance as we gulped down every ounce. We watched the cooling eyes of our little ones with their smiles as the ice cream cascaded from their chins to their clothes. We found ourselves running against the clock. It was already 1:30 in the afternoon and we were scheduled to be at the *curandera's* house by 3:00 p.m. We sprang down the stairs to get to the restrooms, wash away the ice-cream drippings, and prepare for the second part of our journey.

Jamal warned that we still had at least two more hours of driving since Mexicali was one hundred thirteen miles from Tijuana. Within a few minutes, we escaped the congested city traffic and were off to Mexicali. Moved by the thought that I was closer than ever to meeting with the *curandera,* I held Mazen's red shirt and prepared myself for the encounter. I was nervous and on the edge when Jamal said, "We're almost there, but I'm going to stop at the pharmacy down the road so that Amina can double check. I'm sure a lot of people know of the *curandera*."

Her perturbed appearance as she returned from the pharmacy signaled that something was wrong. "We made a wrong turn a few miles back, but it doesn't really matter. We're only thirty minutes away," she said with a grin.

We smiled back at her talking about how we had made a right turn instead of a left one, but compelled by our near arrival wasted no further breath talking about it. We tightened our lips, straightened our backs and prepared for the denouement of our fears.

The *curandera's* house was situated on about half an acre of neglected property. Aside from a few dry plants and an old barn, it gave the impression of an old church. The windows were covered with white curtains thickly gathered, making it impossible to see the interior.

Amina jumped out of the car. I followed quickly. The *curandera* was standing at her front door, gesturing with her hands as though telling us to leave. I looked at Amina and asked what's wrong, what is she saying?

"She said that she doesn't want you to come in. She doesn't understand why you are wearing a black blouse. She will not talk to you as long as you are wearing black."

"Now what do I do? Did I bring myself a curse by wearing black? Jamal? Did I bring my own "Black Curse" with me?" I whimpered.

Jamal looked down on me tenderly. Then, in a soothing tone, one that mothers take with fretful babies, he said, "Follow me."

I followed him to a small white rusted and shabby barn. He took off his white tee shirt and said, "Go in there, take off your blouse and put my tee-shirt on." Dazed by his quick reaction, I did as he said and ran back to the *curandera's* house.

Historical accounts relate the different perspectives of *curanderas* and I knew at that moment that my *curandera* was extramundane. Her belief that the color "black" releases negative energy is supported in color psychology. Black protects and creates a barrier between the external world and ourselves. It hides in the depth of its own agitation while white brings matters to light. In the healer's case, she feared that black might be the catalyst to negatively transform one's entire life and she wanted to make sure that I wore a color that discharged positive, not negative energy. I longed for the *curandera* to transform Mazen's energy in a positive way.

She smiled and said, "Entre," which I assumed, meant, "Enter" or "Welcome to my home." Looking at her fully revealed figure, I perceived her as a heavyset goddess with angelic wings fastened to her shoulders. In a moment, however, wisely judging that one reason she appeared as such was a product of my imagination and the other was her burning blush and resigned smile. Her short, chestnut hair glistening in the sun made her eyebrows appear as if golden threads fastened against her tan-colored skin. Her light green dress seemed to address the attitude of her spirit and the halo of feminine gentility.

We followed her to a room decorated with statues and images of the Virgin Mary and Jesus. There were dry branches of feathery plants exposed near the windowsills and a scent of cinnamon and ginger floating in the air. She ordered me to sit. I told Amina to remind her that Mazen was too ill to join me and that I brought his shirt with me so that she might be able to make a spiritual connection. The *curandera* nodded in agreement. I gave her Mazen's red shirt and sat in silence. Her eyes found mine and then she spoke. Her words did not resonate in my ears. I knew she was communicating with someone or something, but it wasn't with me or Amina. She walked toward the statue of Virgin Mary that was glowing from the flame of over thirty candles and kneeled to the ground. A few minutes later, she stood up and said, *"Rezare por tu hijo,"* and continued to speak to Amina in Spanish.

"Amina, what did she say?" I exclaimed.

Amina's tears made me wonder whether I was going to perish in sorrow or gather back my strength. After I'd realized that the *curandera* felt ashamed at heart that she couldn't give me any *hope*, I stood up, and offered her a hundred dollar bill to thank her for her time. She turned her body away from me while making a *"no"* gesture with her hand. She walked toward the window, looked out for a brief moment, turned around to look me in the eye and lower her gaze. I wanted to learn some detail about why she believed that there was no hope, but I feared I couldn't handle the reality of his fate hiding behind her blank stare. I held myself back from cursing and said nothing.

Shocked to my senses, a shooting headache left me out of breath. I walked out of her home desperate and desolate, only to be faced with the radiant shades of orange and gold as the sun began its departure behind the arid horizon. I began to dread the sunset the way some people dread death.

And what is it to cease breathing, but to free the breath from its restless tides, that it may rise and expand and seek God unencumbered?

—Khalil Gibran

Chapter 14

Walk of Silence

A year after radiation and immunotherapy treatment, Mazen had lost balance and muscle strength due to the increased pressure and the new growth in his brain stem. He was unable to speak clearly. I tried to understand his slurred words, but these were difficult to make sense of and my inquisitive facial expressions fatigued him. Frustrated, he ceased to move his burdened lips and his dimming and bleary eyes became the spectral image of his lost voice.

During this time, I could no longer focus on work and found myself much more at peace while with Mazen. Mona and I called Michigan Hospice and informed the director that we wanted to keep Mazen at home, and we would need assistance. They assigned a nurse, nurse's aide, social worker, and both physical and occupational therapists.

Mona and I took turns watching him on a schedule we devised. The vice-president of the college had given me permission to work mornings from home, so I took the morning shift and my daughters Rania and Dania, my husband Ernie, and my niece Jenny took turns attending to Mazen's needs between noon and four in the afternoon or until Mona came home from work.

We bathed him daily and took care of him as we would a fragile newborn infant. It was difficult to move him because he weighed over two hundred pounds. He wasn't overweight, but at six feet four, he had a powerful, well-built physique. We turned him gently to the right and to the left every two hours to avoid the onset of bedsores. His doctor warned us to watch for them and to be careful not to injure him as we turned him from one side to the other because of the amount of blood thinners in his system.

When Mazen's nurse announced that his organs were failing and that it was just a matter of time before he left this world, I took residence by his bedside. The time had finally come for me to go face-to-face with the enemy and see the dark dilemma of my life made clear.

I looked at Mona, gripping my breast hard as if stricken by a sudden pulse of pain. "A flock of angels will surround Mazen today and we will need to be strong for him."

As she wrestled with my words and her lips were sealed by the phantom of death, she shook her head in confusion and walked away.

Mazen lived in a two-story colonial style home. He'd become bedridden fourteen months after his initial diagnosis, and it was unreasonable to take him up and down the stairs each time we dealt with ambulatory care or had a medical emergency. Mona had cleared out the dining room to set up Mazen's bed and make it easier for everyone to tend to his needs. She aligned a loveseat against the south wall and positioned his bed so he faced east. She positioned it at the time to protect him from the heat of the sun that speared through the door each afternoon. This arrangement was a nice coincidence because in Islam, when a person dies or is nearing death, he or she should face east toward the *Kabaa* or the House of God in Mecca, Saudi Arabia.

Mazen had become yielding and non-responsive to anything we did except when I watched a tear trickle down his cheek in reaction to his six-year-old daughter Yasmine's emotional outbreak.

Yasmine was precocious, alert, and observant for a six-year-old. She knew her father was mortally ill, but it wasn't until the evening before his death that I realized how much she knew. Her siblings Mahmoud, age four, and Jemail, age two, played and ran around while she walked around her father's bed and tugged at the disconnected wires and tubes of the hospital paraphernalia. "Why aren't these connected to Baba anymore?"

I gazed at her. "Come here, sweetheart. Sit on my lap for a minute. Your Baba's not feeling good, and we want you to spend the night with your Aunt Sana. Many of us are going to stay here tonight to make him feel better."

She jumped off my lap and shouted, "No! I'm not going anywhere. I want to stay with Baba." She ran to his bed and climbed up to lie alongside him. She held on to his shirt and said, "I'm staying with him."

Mona picked her up. "No Yasmine, Tata's (Granny's) right. You need to go…" She carried her away.

Yasmine stopped crying for a few seconds. "Can I say good-bye to him before I go?"

We looked at each other and nodded yes simultaneously.

She crawled back up Mazen's bed and stretched her tiny body sideways across his chest. Her curly chestnut hair brushed against his face, and her little arms ran up and down his body.

I looked at Mona and said, "I can't believe this! Does she know that she may never see her father again?"

Everyone in the room was either crying or frozen by her actions. I buried my face in my hands and thought of her arms as vines clinging to her father, a life she feared losing.

I felt as helpless as a dove ready to be sacrificed.

Yasmine continued to cry and sob as she rubbed her cheeks over every inch of Mazen's face and upper body. As soon as her mother approached the bed, Yasmine screamed, "Let me stay! Don't take me away from my Baba!"

Mazen adored Yasmine. She was the sparkle of his life and she knew it.

Mazen had been immobile and non-responsive for months, but his doctor had informed us that hearing would be one of the last senses to lapse before death. We treated him with the utmost respect and spoke to him as though he could hear us even though I did not think that he could focus or absorb what was going on around him because he showed no signs of communication. Yet, immediately after Mona carried Yasmine away, a tear lingered at the corner of his eye as a sign of final adieu. Both he and his little girl knew that the chain of love between them would soon be broken.

I gently navigated the map of time by running my fingers around his eyes and gradually his smooth cheeks. There were no wrinkles, no lines to bridge his youthful face and the rust of old age. I yearned to relive the mother-son bond that gave meaning to my raison d'etre. I thought of his childhood, and wondered if life would ever be the same without him.

Around 9:00 p.m., Theresa, who had left during the day and returned in the evening, took me aside. "I recall that some Muslim families call the priest or *Imam* to read a few prayers when their loved one is nearing the end," she whispered. "Do you want to call one?"

I took a few steps back and stared her directly in the eye. "No, I don't want an Imam. God and His angels are surrounding Mazen and there's no need to call anyone."

Gazing fixedly at the ceiling, I prayed that I was right and that God and His angels were adorning him with their love. Calling the *Imam* would validate Mazen's approaching death, and I wanted to postpone that thought for as long as I could.

To think that this was going to be my last night with Mazen required that I submit to his fate, but I was afraid lest the foundation of my being would collapse, leaving me ill-equipped to put on a traditional veil of passivity and watch him die. I wanted to rebel against humanity and curse my right to live rather than to watch Mazen's innocent face, lighted with purity, transform into shades of blue and gray. I looked at Rania and Dania, who had learned about Mazen's condition from me, and decided to spend the night. I refrained from saying much as I fiddled with the papers and instructions that Theresa had given Mona and me before she left.

The night was long and agonizing. It spoke to me in loud, charging verses, as if a party of spirits had joined hands to dance around Mazen's bed to prepare him for his eternal journey. Oxygen tanks, medical equipment, and chairs surrounded his hospital bed, leaving me very little room to spread a twin-sized air mattress near him. I tried to force fit it between his bed and the loveseat, but there wasn't enough room to stretch my arms and legs. I examined the area connecting the dining room to the living room and placed my mattress at the bottom of Mazen's bed. It made it easier for others to get to him without having to step over the mattress. Mona lay on the loveseat, Dania took the recliner, and Rania slept on the couch near the front window of the living room. Despite all the preparations, we gazed at each other, wondering if any of us would actually fall asleep.

Surrounded by pillows, I curled up and prayed that my rib cage would hold hostage the ruins of my remaining *hope*. I tossed and turned and tried to close my eyes, an impossibility. I asked Mona for more pillows so that I could prop myself up to see Mazen's face. I wanted to watch him breathe. But before Theresa retired for the night, she'd said, "Mazen's heart rate for the moment is in the normal range, and he might make it through the night. But to facilitate his breathing, give him one milliliter of morphine every fifteen minutes. Call me if things get complicated."

As anticipated, none of us could sleep. Mona and I set the timer and each time it went off, we took turns administering the morphine. I stared occasionally at the oxygen tank propped in the far right corner of the room. It stood between his bed and the north wall of the dining room. Theresa didn't think Mazen would need it, but I rehearsed the steps of its usage to avoid last-minute panic in case she was wrong. I didn't want death to make its way through. I wasn't ready to let Mazen go.

When we spoke, we whispered. My battle with death was ending. It wasn't going to be a *walk of silence, but* rather *a walk of clamor and remonstrance.*

I stood strong as I fought Mazen's battle, but I was getting weaker by the day, and I wasn't sure that I could keep my calm any further. I had struggled for twenty long months until his inevitable fate lingered in my heart's chambers, waiting for a moment to strike. Watching him die was more than heartrending; it felt as if the entire human race had expired. I held my breath each time I saw his chest rise and fall. I sensed even though he couldn't open his eyelids to see me for lack of muscle strength, he could hear every word I said.

Mona and I clutched his hands, hoping they would stay warm. Around 2:00 a.m., I fell asleep for a few minutes and woke up disturbed. I imagined Mazen hovering in the air like a glimmering star that seemed suddenly to vanish without trace. My mind quivered with a fear compounded by sorrow and tendered with divine intervention.

Mazen was going to die and I was frantically alarmed each time I observed his chest remain still for more than five seconds. I thought that by reading hospice booklets and listening to my daughter Dania tell me about her chat room conversations with families who had lost their loved ones from brain tumors it would help prepare me for Mazen's passage, but instead, I felt the gnawing teeth of death eating away at my skin.

Dania stood upright, dragged her feet as she walked toward me, sat on the floor next to my mattress, and shared one of her chat room stories, hoping to comfort me.

I plugged my ears and screamed, "Please stop! I don't want to hear it because Mazen is different. God will have mercy on him until the very end. Sitting on coals of fire and fearing the unknown is destroying me. Comparing him to others isn't going to make me feel better."

"I was just trying to help," Dania muttered as she picked herself up and walked back to the other side of the room with tears streaming down her face.

I wish I had stuffed a rag in my mouth before yelling at her and hurting her feelings. The echo of her soft voice pierced my bones. I buried my face in my hands and wept. The room went silent.

My mind stayed weary as Mona and Rania broke the silence and occupied themselves by whispering to each other or by lifting Mazen's head with more pillows to make sure he was comfortable. I couldn't blot out the haunting feeling that played nonstop upon my senses, caused by hurting Dania's feelings. I lifted myself to my feet, walked across the room, and sat near her. She was weeping tears of grief as she reclined on her brother's favorite chair. I hugged her tight. With tear-filled eyes, I summoned the courage to speak to her. "Dania, I feel selfish and thick-minded. Please don't be mad at me."

"I'm not," Dania answered, staring at her lap.

"Dania, I'm hurting because Mazen may be different. Brain tumors affect people in different ways and all the literature depicting the final phases of life could be meaningless and misleading. Mazen has a strong heart."

I went back to my mattress talking to myself... Maybe this isn't the end... Maybe I'm losing my mind...I don't know why I feel this way. Maybe she's facing reality, and I'm the one in denial. Who knows...? I thought of Mazen's neurologist. Each time I called him, he would say, "Mazen has a strong heart..." and I would think...Did he really want to say... *Oh, you mean he's still alive? Maybe he is really going to die . . . Will he suffocate the way his father did?*

When Mahmoud was ill, Mazen and I had told the doctors that knowing Mahmoud, he would not want to be resuscitated or to lie in a vegetative state indefinitely. We thought that when he neared the end, his chest would rattle for a few seconds, and his heart would stop. It would be like a streak of lightening followed by thunder. We were wrong. Mazen was still in school when his father died. The doctor had come out to get me from the family room. I threw up my arms and ran with a mighty strength. My cheeks flushed and the inside of my head was rioting against the normal flow of blood, like throwing salt on an ulcerated wound. It was 2:45 in the afternoon, around the time when our chauffeur picked my children up from school and dropped them off at the hospital. I prayed they would be held up in traffic. I didn't want them to witness the fierceness of their father's death and its manifestation on the physicians and nurses surrounding him.

Mahmoud gasped for breath and waved his arms toward me repeatedly for what seemed like eternity. He begged me to save him. I felt guilty and desperate. I was breathing hard and looking in all directions. One of the attending physicians suggested that I leave the room, but I couldn't. I grew cold and my stomach turned as I watched him take his last breath. One could never be prepared for such a moment. I shivered with a cold that penetrated my bones.

I feared that Mazen too, might gasp for breath during his final moments, and I had mentioned my apprehension to his nurse. She assured me that with the amount of morphine that he would receive, he wasn't going to gasp for breath. I believed her.

I looked at his vital signs around 7:00 a.m. and his heart rate read 92. I took my car keys, told Mona that I was going home to take a shower and change and that I'd be back twenty minutes later. My daughters, who also lived minutes away, left to do the same.

Exhausted from living with the burden of losing Mazen, I felt like tearing the earth apart with my bare hands. I ran to my car, circling around the lamppost as fast as I could. Then I turned on the ignition, stepped on the gas, and drove down the street with hope that I wouldn't run into traffic. I squinted to stay alert.

As much as I hated cold showers, I knew that it would be the only way to feel cleansed and refreshed. I dashed through the house and jumped into the shower. Within a few minutes, I felt uplifted.

When I realized that ten minutes had passed, I dressed quickly. On my way out, my husband Ernie yelled, "Hey...you put your blouse on inside out!"

I didn't look down to double check. I took him for his word, and changed it around while running toward the garage. I felt regretful about having left Mazen. I prayed.

Then, when Mona greeted me with an expression of friendliness, I knew he was still breathing. I approached his bed and took his hand. It felt warm and comforting. Rania and Dania walked in behind me. We took turns holding his hand and calling on God to continue to protect him.

My mother was among the first of our morning visitors. She walked in and said, "I wonder who's going to die, you or Mazen. Did you get any sleep?"

"Ma! Does it matter?"

She walked around to hug me, sat in the corner, and pulled out her tissues to wipe away her tears and sniffles. She loved and respected my son, but her shadowy form of grief made me wonder if she was hurting more over me than over Mazen.

As I caressed Mazen's hand and arm, I wanted, finally. to say to him, *I love you... I miss our conversations...* but I couldn't. I was afraid that my words would scare him and the last thing I wanted was for him to be afraid.

I was confused. I wondered if I really would see him again. *If he died, where would he go? What is the afterlife like? Would he wait for me in purgatory? Is purgatory real? I felt the urge to talk to an Imam, a priest, a rabbi, anyone who could tell me where Mazen would go.*

I let go of his hand, walked over to an empty chair, buttressed my forehead against my hands and pressed hard. I wanted the throbbing of my temples to vanish and the noises in my head to disappear. *I wish I had a brain tumor. Why him, not me? Was I going to scream when his heart stopped? Would I be able to control my emotions? Does it matter?* I sat on the chair facing Mazen's feeble body and thought of a horrifying dream I'd had two weeks before Mazen's diagnosis.

I saw an unfamiliar, heavy-set woman dressed in white. Her dress covered her entire body. It was like the long sleeve nightgowns that my grandmother used to wear before she slipped beneath her white quilted comforter. A thin, translucent scarf wrapped loosely around the woman's black hair. She might have been in her mid-fifties, but

*her age was hard to discern because of her expressionless face. If she
had any wrinkles, they were certainly hidden behind the tension that
masked her rounded cheeks and lips. She stared at me while sitting
motionless on a bench about thirty feet from where I stood frozen.
I waited for her to make a move, afraid of her fixed stare and of the
huge, black snake that quietly coiled on her lap. She beckoned me to
come to her. She lifted the snake with her large arms and motioned
for me to relieve her of her burden. She insisted that I take it from
her by repeatedly lifting the snake and urging me with her hands to
walk toward her. As I continued to observe her in silence, gazing into
the core of her being, trying to make sense of what she was doing, I
imagined a ghost. She wasn't someone I knew and she appeared to
be on a mission. I felt afraid to turn away without carrying out her
charge. The vibrations between us informed me that I would save
her by taking the snake. I wondered . . .who sent her on this mission?
Why is she in my dream?*

*Taken aback, I thought of my past and the bitter taste of death. I
already knew what it was like to lose a loved one and I didn't want
something so dreadful to happen again, especially if she and her
snake had someone I loved in mind.*

*I wanted to run, but my legs were paralyzed. As I allowed the
distance and light between us to dwarf me, I floated backward and
screamed, "Never will I touch that snake. It's yours! Get away from
me! Go away! Never come back!" She ignored my pleas and insisted
that I take it from her. I screamed louder and louder . . .*

My husband, who was lying next to me, shook my arm. "Wake
up! Whatever it was, you'll be all right. You're safe now."

He draped me in his arms and squeezed. I pulled away and began
to reflect on the horrific meaning of my dream. I didn't want to be
comforted when analytical thinking was my priority.

I wasn't sure what to make of my dream. My facial muscles grew
tight, and I felt pain in my jaw from grinding my teeth. I massaged
my jaw, jumped out of bed, opened the drawer of my nightstand, and
removed the dream book from beneath a small book filled with an
assortment of precious verses about mothers. I froze for a moment

and thought . . . Mazen had given me that tiny book, named *For Mother,* on Mother's Day of that same year. I held it in my palm for a few seconds, set it aside, and opened the *Dictionary of Dreams* and read about my predicted fate.

Do I believe in dream symbols? Yes. It seems that all of my dreams come true and I knew that this dream was bound to lead to a large misfortune. I read, *"To dream of snakes is a foreboding of evil in its various forms and stages."*

I stopped reading and began to cry. Ernie tried to console me by saying, "It was just a dream."

But I knew better. *Nothing is ever just a dream.* I thought of Mazen and his headaches and I prayed God wouldn't try me again. I assumed that He only tries us once in life, and I was certainly not ready for a second trial, not now, not ever. I also knew that I could not change destiny. If something were critically wrong with Mazen, I knew that this time, I wouldn't fight God; I would join Him and pray for mercy.

I couldn't sleep. I thought of the worst while peering out the window at the edge of dawn, sipping on coffee. The black snake...

The inner world of grief felt personal. It was as though my grief was engulfed by the vastness of the Earth and nothing was left, but the thunder of dead voices rolling over the plains, swimming over the oceans, and swarming over the skies. I looked around and wondered...why me? Am I alone? Why is it that those around me cannot see or hear my pain? I was bitter. I was resentful. I didn't know why, but I became angry even at those who tried to comfort me. I prayed that my days would turn into nights so that I could dig up the earth to retrieve my memories of Mazen, memories that seemed entwined with visions of blissful thoughts and dreadful dreams. If someone placed their hand on my shoulder to reassure me that all would be fine, I became mute from fear of saying the wrong thing because I knew—I would never be fine. No matter how hard I tried to conceal my anger, it surfaced like a savage beast in the middle of nowhere. I tried hard to gather the strength I needed to nestle with what was left of my life, but I felt like my breath had been sucked away by the dark spirits of the sea.

Anger is a necessary stage . . . Be willing to feel your anger, even though it may seem endless. The more you truly feel it, the more it will begin to dissipate and the more you will heal. . . anger is just another indication of the intensity of your love.

—David Kessler and Elizabeth Kubler Ross
On Grief and Grieving, 2005

Chapter 15

The Death Trap

After dawn, friends and family members began to pour into Mazen's home. I went to the kitchen to get a cup of coffee, took a sip and poured it in the sink. I wasn't sure if the cloak of death wrapping itself around my taste buds was the bitter taste of coffee or the bitter taste of life.

A friend approached me with a capsule of Prozac. "Take it. It'll help you feel better," she insisted.

"Thank you, but I need to be strong for him, not weak," I said with a sigh. "The pill will make me feel weak and helpless. I'd rather smoke a cigarette than to feel inwardly paralyzed."

As unconscious as Mazen appeared at 8:15 a.m., a slight movement of his left hand led me to think that he wanted me to hold it as he left this world. I held it and wept with hope that he wouldn't hear my sniffles. By 9:15, his breathing became shallow. Contrary to what the nurses said, morphine didn't stop him from gasping for breath. He had difficulty breathing for at least five minutes.

I looked at his nurse and raised my hands in panic. "What's

happening? Speak to me. Oh no! He's not breathing! I looked at his eyelids. They were still. "He's gone! No! No! No!" I screamed as I collapsed over him.

The haunting face of death had conquered Mazen. He was thirty-three years old and he died on *Good Friday*. I wanted to believe that this was a coincidence, but deep down I knew that this was a powerful message from God reassuring me that he went to better place.

I heard myself wailing, saying words I recalled an elderly Arab women reciting at funerals. I circled around Mazen's peaceful face, touching it with my fingers and pressing my lips against it. I ran my hand gently over his forehead hoping that it would stay warm. I kissed it time after time while running my fingers across his eyes and his cheeks. All I could hear myself say was, *Mazen . . .what about me? How come you didn't take me with you? You always think of me. Why did you leave me now? Please don't go. I want to be in your place. Why didn't you let me take your place?*

I turned my face to God in despair and said, "God, please take me to him, please!"

The face that had been pale for so long vanished like a star that imploded in the distance between Earth and sky. The weight of not seeing it anymore fell upon my shoulders like a strange phantom. He was a handsome young man, his eyes large, black, and olive shaped. They had sparkled behind his thick, black eyelashes, making one wonder if eyes alone could smile. His fine features had crystalized over the years, like spring renewing its youth to coax out the smiles of lovers, or a summer sun shedding its glory upon all. His small, delicate nose and his lips protruded below a black and neatly trimmed mustache. The dimple on his right cheek had accentuated his natural smile that always seemed a conversation opener. I looked closely at his peaceful and motionless face and prayed that it would retain its pinkish-pale skin tone, and that the oxygen bearing blood would somehow continue to flow through his veins.

Each time someone touched me and told me not to cry and to let him go, I'd pull myself away and say, "No! You have no right to tell me what to do or what to say. He's my son and I have every right to cry and to say what I want."

Then, when a woman I had never seen before told me to stop crying, I turned to the other people in the room. "If there's anyone here who thinks he or she has the right to tell me what to do, please leave now. I'm tired of being told that I cannot cry. Leave me alone. Please!"

A few seconds later, I looked at their troubled faces and said, "I'm sorry," collapsing on the loveseat near Mazen's bed.

My brother Jamal took me in his arms. "I have to call the medics so they can take him to the funeral home," he whispered. "Mazen needs to be washed and buried by tomorrow morning. You know the tradition. He should be buried within twenty-four hours."

I jumped back and screamed, "No, Jamal, not now. Please give me some time with him."

With tears rolling down his cheeks, he replied, "Take as much time as you need," and he stepped outside.

Within an hour, I realized that there was no way around the inevitable and that Mazen's presence was causing too much pain to Mona and my daughters. I kissed his cheek to devour the taste of death and walked to the kitchen to sip on a cup of juice. The aroma of coffee filled the air and filtered through my nostrils. A half hour later, a young man, perhaps one of Mazen's friends, saw me staring at the coffee pot and offered me a cup. I thanked him, tested the richness of coffee creamer, and went to my brother Jamal. "I'm ready now. You can call the funeral home."

I was too grief-stricken to watch the funeral home people carry him away, but I still felt the urge to wish him farewell. I could feel God's angels surrounding him. As much as I felt there was no reality in the face of death, I knew the angels were present. I had felt them when Mahmoud died, and I sensed that they girdled the contours of Mazen's bed immediately before they took his soul. They were like gray shadows of light roaming around his feet, preparing him for his eternal flight. I wasn't prepared either to reveal what I'd seen or to deal with the elongated faces and teary eyes of the people who might think that I'd gone insane. I had learned over the years to keep what I saw of the mystical world to myself.

When the medics arrived, they came in the back patio. They entered through the kitchen and walked into the dining room. They began to remove Mazen's medical paraphernalia and prepared to place him in a body bag. I jumped from my seat and said, "No! Don't touch him. We've been treating him with tender love and care throughout his illness and you are not going to bag him away as though he were a *sprinkle of dust.*"

My sister Samerah stood next me and said, "You're right. We won't let them do that." She whispered something in her sons' ears. Ronnie and Haitham moved toward me as though taking their first steps. Then Ronnie held my hand and walked me to the opposite side of the room. "I'll take care of Mazen. Don't worry. I won't let them put him in a body bag."

I felt relieved. I let go of his grasp.

I could not see what was happening. Samerah took me out the front the door to walk me around the house and give her sons more time to place Mazen on a stretcher. When Ronnie signaled to her that they were ready, we walked toward the patio to comfort their broken hearts and watch them lift him away.

Watching Mazen's removal from his home and waving him adieu was the last time I felt a genuine connection to this world, as though a part of me was also lifted from this world to one of immortality where only the dead could communicate. A naked feeling possessed with fire, the same kind of feeling that seizes you when you're angry and you want to ignite the world with the white flame of your breath. I drifted...I felt numb...

I couldn't fathom that Mazen was gone and that I was actually going to bury him. I wanted to see him and hold him in my arms at least one more time. I asked my mother if I could join the men in the cleansing rituals at the funeral home. She said, "Mothers don't share in the cleansing process and you can see him in the evening once they're done."

Someone inserted the Quran CD into Mazen's stereo player. The words of God resonated in my ears and took me on a spiritual journey of Quranic analysis. Eventually the words became nerve-racking and confusing. I was on a hopeless search of some clue to the whereabouts of Mazen. My concentration was interrupted when my granddaughter Yasmine came running at me. She re-opened my wounds with her hugs and tears, screaming, "I want my *Baba*."

I held her in my arms and wondered…*was there a verse in the Quran that alluded to this? Will she ever see her Baba again?* I wasn't sure and vowed at that very moment to read and reread the entire Quran until I found what I was looking for. I thought of the day Mazen was born and how I had vowed to protect him until the day I died.

My Aunt Khadija, who had moved from Africa to the United States to spend the rest of her life with my mother and her two brothers, walked through the door to pay her condolences. She was my absentee mother while I lived in Africa. She'd mothered my mother, who was seven years her junior and now, me. She held me in her arms and pulled me against her bosom. I sobbed while inhaling the sweet aroma of her inflamed spirit.

Mazen was gone. The seven-day memorial services would be held at his home, and his burial was scheduled at noon the following day, since Islam recommends a speedy burial. Each time I left his home, I'd drive away not knowing where to go. I envisioned the skies would open and I'd disappear into a vacuum of dust.

Chapter 16

Wrapped in White

Peace, my heart, let the time for the parting be sweet.
Let it not be a death but completeness.

—RABINDRANATH TAGORE

I collapsed on the large green metal lounge chair on the back deck of Mazen's home and told those who were surrounding me with hugs to leave me alone. I needed time to process his death in the deep mysterious ocean of my faith. I questioned all death's wily ways while trying not to hear or to see the shadowy secrets of my black dream. My grief embraced my spirit, leaving me very little room to make sense of Mazen's death or even attempt to accept it. The chair I rested on began to feel like it was made of rose thorns that pierced every inch of my body.

Suddenly, I jumped. I looked at my watch. It was 4:15 p.m. My husband and brothers were at the funeral home, participating in the Muslim ritual of washing, shrouding, and praying over Mazen's corpse to prepare him for his burial. Muslims wash (*ghusl*) the dead by following certain rules and procedures, and the body can only be washed by Muslims familiar with *ghusl* guidelines. Women are not allowed to join the men at the funeral home until the washing is complete and the body is wrapped and prepared for the grave. According to Islam, Mazen would be shrouded in a *kafan* or white cotton cloth, a sign of humility, before being placed in the casket. The Quran states that humans are a product of earth; it is to earth that they shall return.

Around eight in the evening, Jamal called me. With a catch in his voice, he said, "We're done. You can come and see him if you want."

"Okay, I'm on my way."

I took my purse and motioned at Mona and my daughters to join me. I stepped out on the porch, looked at the clouded sky, and realized that my somber feelings had become garmented by the remnant of a former life, a lifeless life that was waiting for me at the funeral home. Silenced by an inarticulate breath and moved by the shuddering terror reflected in the faces of my passengers, I drove away.

I was doused in cold guilt as I looked at Mazen's angelic face, wishing it were me laying there. The white shroud covered his body and his head, with room for his large eyes to move into the emptiness of my heart. They were sending out vibrations of a wordless conversation bursting forth through the whole ugliness of death. I yearned to find the strength to rise above the mystery of death and to speak to Mazen's tender face, a face prepared to glorify God through the gated world of eternity. The white wrap took me back to the day I held Mazen in my arms for the first time, his aroma fresh and sweet. He was draped in the white wrap that enveloped his fragile body to protect his tiny limbs, my bundle of joy.

* * *

I was sixteen when Mazen was born on July 24, 1967. I was living in Dakar, Senegal at the time, and as an American, I assumed that I would be treated with respect in a hospital setting, but not so, in this semi-African, semi-French hospital. Two male aides rushed me on a stretcher to the surgical unit and directed my husband and aunt to go to the family waiting room.

"Shut up or I'll shut you up," said the French nurse whose upper arm, covered with a thick, oval seven-inch patch of black-haired mole, led me to believe she was some form of human animal rushing at me from the jungles of Africa. I stopped and stared at her for a brief moment, but as the pain rose anew, I screamed, "Get away from me! I want my mother!"

Upon hearing this, she slapped me across the face with every ounce of strength she had and promised me encores. I touched my stinging face, looked at her with a scowl, and screamed even louder.

She called the anesthesiologist and told him, "Knock her out now so the doctor can start cutting the baby out of her womb. We don't think the baby is alive, but if it is, we're running out of time."

"What does that mean? What are you going to do to me?" I yelled.

"Listen, big baby, I'm not your mother. I'm your nurse! You be quiet and do as we say!"

I turned quickly to the doctor whose short, chubby arms and cold expression as he watched over the live movie of my torture and delivery made me wonder if he were some frozen animal from the Ice Age. I said, "Please help me!"

He gave me a stern look. "I'm not sure if you understand what we are telling you or if the anesthesia is working as quickly as we'd hoped, but I'm losing patience and if you don't stop screaming, I'm going to cut you open now!"

His words confirmed my assumption of his barbaric qualities and I immediately jumped off the operating table.

Two African males who looked more like bodyguards than nursing assistants ran toward me from the corner of the room, grabbed me by the arms and legs, and placed me back on the hard, cold table. They tied my wrists to the table's railings and turned toward the nurse as if to say, *What next?*

As my screams became louder, the nurse, who had totally lost patience, ran toward me and slammed a mask full of ether against my nose to knock me out.

I woke up drowsy and in pain. My mouth was dry and I was thirsty. As I lifted my head to see if someone were around, I shouted, "My stomach! It hurts."

With tears streaming down my cheeks, my mother's sister, whom I referred to as *Khalti,* was sitting on a brown, wooden chair lined up alongside my bed. She held my hand and said, "You'll be fine, sweetheart. You had a C-section and thank God your baby boy is alive . . ."

Baby? Alive? My baby? Am I actually a mother? Can I see my baby? My pain interrupted my thoughts and I started crying again. I turned to *Khalti* and said, "Can I please have a glass of water?"

"Nope!" she shouted, shaking her head sideways. "I can't give you any water. That can be very dangerous after surgery. I'll wet your lips with this ice cube. I wrapped it in large gauze so that you can hold onto it whenever you feel your lips are dry."

"But I want to drink! I want to drink now!"

She stood up, looked me in the eye, and said in a firm and formal tone, "I'm sorry, but I have to go by the doctor's orders. Maybe tomorrow...maybe the day after...we'll see."

Khalti's presence reminded me of my baby, a baby that I hadn't even seen. It reminded me of how she had guessed I was pregnant when I'd visited her eight months earlier. When I described to her how I felt nauseous and drowsy all the time, she smiled and said, "Congratulations! You must be pregnant." I had missed my December period. I was supposed to have it a week before my sixteenth birthday. I thought to myself... *maybe she's right.*

I studied my aunt when I first saw her. I studied her towering height, how she dressed, how she raised her children, treated her husband, and even how she smoked her cigarettes. Sometimes she'd light up two cigarettes thinking she'd already smoked the first one. I'd laugh and tell her; "*Khalti,* you forgot about this one." She'd hug me tight and say, "I hope you never pick up the habit."

"Oh, I won't"—but by the time I was twenty, I was smoking a

pack a day. I loved *Khalti;* she was kind to me. She favored me over her daughters and treated me like a crystal bowl filled with the jewels of her sister and two brothers in America. She hadn't seen them for decades. I was her only connection, at least for the moment.

I'd had conflicting feelings about my pregnancy. Even though I was scared, I imagined myself cradling a baby with gentleness. I wanted to hold it in my arms and hope that it would be the blessing of my life and that the child would harvest its passion through the power of my love. But I also feared the unknown, the unborn nakedness of tomorrow.

The pregnancy had gone smoothly, but at thirty-two weeks, I began to lose amniotic fluid. Out of naivety, I thought that I was wetting my panties because I ate too much watermelon the night before. I shared the information with my late husband, Mahmoud, who was equally naive. We took the matter lightly. That same evening, *Khalti* had come to visit me and when I told her what was happening, without hesitation she said, "You're in labor. Losing amniotic fluid is like taking a fish out of water. Get ready to have your baby."

I was in a total panic. She and Mahmoud rushed me to a private clinic where the midwife insisted on examining me. I had never been examined before, and I was very uncomfortable with the idea. *Khalti* raised her voice and said still with a cold composure, "You better let her examine you or you may lose that baby!" It took me fifteen minutes to take off my panties, but the doctor was patient and acted busy with paperwork. When I finally told her that I was ready, she examined me and said, "You're dilating and to be safe, you need to check in and remain under observation."

I checked in the same evening, but once Mahmoud and *Khalti* left, I began to wrestle with fear and my emotions. I tossed and turned with hope that my baby would miraculously leave my womb and settle in my arms. I was frustrated and left the clinic three days later. I was only thirty-five weeks pregnant. I hoped to delay the baby's birth.

After two days of rest at home, I woke up screaming in the middle of the night from the sharp pain running through my spine. I jumped out of bed and told Mahmoud. Not sure what to do, we called *Khalti* who was staying with my sister-in-law, a very close friend of hers.

"Pick me up now," she yelled. "If something happens to my niece, my sister will never forgive me."

Back at the clinic, the midwife who examined me said that I had begun to dilate, but that she could barely hear the baby's heartbeat. She and the doctor on call strongly recommended a C-section.

Khalti shouted with a tremor in her voice. "No! My neighbor's daughter had a C-section last week and she died. I'm afraid of C-sections!"

"Mahmoud, take her to the main hospital. We need a second opinion. What if she doesn't need surgery?"

"My nose! It hurts," I cried.

I remembered how the nurse threatened me prior to my surgery and instructed to stop screaming before she smacked my nose with an ether mask. I hated her.

"*Khalti,* I'm in pain. My stomach hurts. Please do something."

Early in my pregnancy, I wondered whether the foreign object inside of me was something that I really wanted. I was always depressed and could not understand why the changes in my body were making me feel fat and ugly. I tried to conceal my pregnancy under my clothing because I didn't want anyone to notice my swelling body. It wasn't very difficult to do since I didn't have any friends. Mahmoud didn't know how to drive, so I was home most of the time. On weekends, Mahmoud would go with his best friend to the beach, or go to visit with other male friends. He'd installed a hinge hasp on the outside of the apartment door to lock me in with a padlock when he left home on the weekends.

"I'm locking you in because I'm afraid you might leave the apartment and get lost. Get yourself some rest while I'm gone. I'll be back before dark. Believe me."

Not accustomed to being secluded from society, I felt like I was living an ugly dream. I didn't know how to measure what he'd said. My idea of right was his idea of wrong, but I trained myself to accept his right and reject my wrong while tears of my shattered spirit transformed into the chains of my oppression. I touched my stomach and wondered about the life that was floating inside me and prayed that it would be sweeter than laughter and greater than boredom.

To avoid thinking about why I couldn't join him, I played the stereo. The only record I had was *Nights in White Satin* by the Moody Blues. I played it over and over until I memorized the lyrics. I closed my eyelids and drifted into the world of music. My loneliness and pain merged as I sang with the artist and wept in the dragging darkness of its lyrics.

I took a deep breath and was startled by Khalti's hand shaking my shoulder and saying, "Were you asleep? Are you okay?"

"Oh yes. I'm better. Khalti, do I really have a baby boy? What's his name? Did they give him a name?"

"Yes," she replied. "His name is Mazen."

"Mazen? I've never heard the name before. Who named him? What does the name mean?"

"Oh, I don't know. Your brother-in-law Ali named him. He reads a lot about Arab history. He said that Mazen B. Ghadubah was a distinguished Muslim figure and that an entire tribe was named after him. He was the first individual from Southeast Arabia to accept Islam."

"Whatever. Can I see him? Please…?" I replied, left to her mercy.

"Listen, if you can help yourself heal by thinking about your wound, they might move you out of the surgical unit and into the maternity ward. Then maybe, they will bring him to you. How's that? Let's work on getting you better. I don't want anything to happen to you now. Your mother trusted me with you, and I have to live up to her expectations. I can't let anything bad happen to you. You know what I mean?"

"Yes, I do," I said with a straight face.

Two days later, I was moved to the maternity ward and Mahmoud, who was extremely excited, visited me in the evenings. Each time he visited, he filled the room with roses and chocolates. He poured change into the drawer of the nightstand. "This is so you can tip the nurse's aides when they do their rounds."

I promised him that I would, but before he left, I said, "Wait, can I see Mazen? When can I see him? Is he all right?"

"Oh yes, he's fine," Mahmoud said as he walked out the door.

As I glanced out the window the following morning, I noticed that other patients were walking around in their robes or resting on benches, catching the sun's rays and rubbing their eyes occasionally to clear their vision from the beaming sun. Out of curiosity, I decided to join them. I stood up, grabbed my robe, and. stepped out of my room into a wide, beautifully tiled floor. I immediately realized that walking was overwhelming and that I had to move slowly. My eyes focused on the white, blue, and green patterns of the ceramic tile beneath my feet. I was afraid that I might trip and I couldn't even fathom what it might feel like to add more pain to my healing incision.

I carefully stepped down into the garden and was able to see the uniqueness of the facility. The hospital was like an ancient resort. During my afternoon walks, I found myself surrounded by an array of colorful flower gardens and trees. The scent of jasmine and roses tickled my nostrils each afternoon as I stood smiling at the splendor of sunshine. I lifted my chin to expose my face in tranquil delight to the glittering sun, hoping to burn away its paleness.

The large, two-story villas serving as wards were separated four to five hundred feet apart from each other. The intensive care unit was situated to the left of the maternity ward and the neonatal unit was to its right. I contemplated jumping the fence to reach the neonatal ward and get a glimpse of Mazen, but I was too weak. The wound from the C-section was oozing and causing discomfort. I carried my agony in silence and took advantage of the soothing scenery. I was told that I had to spend a total of ten days in the hospital.

I spent most of my mornings reading magazines and my afternoons walking among the flowerbeds and the exotic plants that decorated the landscape with patterns of green and yellow shades. I'd carefully step over the small patches of low-maintenance grass to avoid damaging the environment. When I was tired of walking, I'd settle on a small, gracefully crafted white bench to gaze at the birds as they perched and sang to each other across the flowering branches.

After six days of pleading with Khalti and Mahmoud to see Mazen, I realized that my supplications were pointless. On the seventh day, I grabbed the nurse's aide's hand after she had finished bathing me and placed it in the drawer of my nightstand that Mahmoud had filled with change. I said, "You can take all the money in this drawer if you can bring me my son."

She looked at the money for a split second and said, "What's your son's name?"

"It's Mazen," I said in a soft tone.

She looked at me with compassion and said, "All right! I'll be right back."

I couldn't believe that she might return with Mazen. My mouth was dry with anticipation and my lips quivered as I listened to my own voice repeat the words, please, please, please bring him. After ten minutes of what felt like a lifetime, I feared the unknown. *Had everyone been lying to me? Was Mazen real?*

I waited.

"Here he is…he's all yours. He's no longer in the incubator, so I don't want him to be missed."

Mazen was wrapped in white with only his face exposed. It glowed behind the contours of the white cotton swaddle that dressed his body like an arm brace would support a broken arm. I took a deep breath, exhaled in slow motion, and lifted Mazen from her arms to mine. The blanket felt soft and fuzzy. I no longer struggled to find out if he was alive. His heartbeat resonated against my chest. Mazen was mine. It was hard to believe that I didn't have to share him as I did my brother Jamal when mother claimed him. This tiny little bundle was in my possession, and I vowed to protect and shield it from harm for as long as I lived.

His little bracelet read Mazen Saleh—2.2 kg—24/7/1967.

I whispered in his ear, "Mazen, you are so tiny, so beautiful, so innocent…I love you more than life."

I was suddenly startled by the aide's shouting. "Madame, Madame! Give him back to me. I need to take him back now!"

"Of course. I didn't realize that ten minutes had already gone by. Take him. Be careful, oh...and please take the money. Thank you very much for bringing him to me. Will you bring him again tomorrow?" I said anxiously.

She ignored my request and rushed him back to the nursery.

When Mahmoud visited me that evening, I told him that I'd seen Mazen and was hoping that I could take him and go home.

"You can go home in a few days. What do you think? Does he look like you or me? I think he looks like you," he exclaimed.

"Oh, I don't know. He might still change a lot," I said as I looked out the window. Three days later, I left the hospital with Mazen in my arms. I looked forward to being his mother. I smiled so much all the way home, my face hurt.

Mazen was two weeks old, and I cared for him with intense and concentrated focus. He had become the center of my life. I tried to breastfeed him, but I had no milk. Mahmoud bought me canned milk from the Alpine mountains. We hoped that it would increase my lactation. My efforts were mocked by Mazen's piercing hunger cries. I ceased to breastfeed.

I wasn't sure I had enough knowledge or understanding of my mission as a mother, but I did my best to follow the advice of neighbors and relatives. Their words, "Feed him every three hours no matter how much he cries" rang in my ears like an outcry that went pealing through the night. But they never talked to me about malnutrition, fever, or diarrhea. I was proud of myself. I thought I knew it all until a visit from my sister-in-law proved me wrong.

When Zainab called to tell me that she was coming over, I wanted to make sure everything was just right. She was my mother's friend, and I wanted to impress her. I told the housekeeper to prepare some sweets and coffee. When Zainab arrived, I said, "Would you like to hold him?"

She glanced at her burgundy silk blouse and her puffy long sleeves and said, "Yes, I'll hold him. Why not?"

I smiled.

"Wait a minute. Did you realize that this baby is hot? He's very hot. He needs a doctor.

"My heart sank upon hearing her words." A doctor? Why?"

"I'll explain later. I'm taking this baby to a doctor now!" She darted out the door.

"Wait, wait. I'm coming with you.

She walked toward the elevator and said, "Hurry up! Come on!"

I grabbed my purse and bumped into the housekeeper as she walked toward me with the coffee tray.

"Forget the coffee! The sweets! Something's wrong with Mazen! I need to leave!"

She stood for a split second and leaped away.

"Is this the mother?" Stiffened with aversion, the doctor said as he looked at me. I felt like a criminal. "The baby has an ear infection and he needs antibiotics. Take his temperature on the hour, and if it goes over 40 degrees centigrade, bring him back here or go to emergency."

"*Merci*," I said, looking at him with a vacant gaze. I bundled Mazen in my arms feeling as though I'd committed a sin and should stand on a pedestal of shame. By the time I walked out of the doctor's office, Mazen had fallen asleep.

I patted *Zainab* on the shoulder and said, "Please go home. Mazen is going to be fine. I learned a lesson today. Thank you for educating me."

She smiled, "No, I'm not leaving yet. I will go with you to fill his prescription, and I will walk you home."

I cuddled him against my chest and whispered, "What a relief... Mazen. You're going to be fine."

Exhausted but deeply content that I'd overcome my first test of motherhood, I read Dr. Spock's *Baby and Child Care,* a book that my sister Samerah had carefully packaged among the numerous gifts she and my mother had sent me when Mazen was born. She had written me a note that she had carefully placed between the layers of clothes advising me to read the book. I followed her advice with the wavering arms of a desperate mother each time I noticed that Mazen did or experienced something that fell out of the norm. My love for Mazen grew stronger by the day and I was constantly watching over him and searching for traces of strange behavior or unusual facial expressions. I protected him from everyone, even other children, family members, and neighbors. I watched over him with my whole soul, fearing to ignore a singular circumstance that fell out of the ordinary.

I took a deep breath and startled by my mother's hand tapping my shoulder, I came back to the reality of the funeral home. I wanted to scream and jump out the window, but I felt weak.

"Are you okay?"

"I'm okay. I'll live. It's Mazen that I want. I want him back, Ma. Where's Daddy? He knows all about God, life, and death. He's read the Quran a million times. Can he tell me where Mazen is? I want Mazen back. Please Ma! Please!"

I wondered if I could have sheltered Mazen from the toxic pollution of bombs while we had lived in war-torn Lebanon. I wondered if I had taken him to a doctor to be x-rayed early on in life; if I had pressured him not to smoke; if I had prayed more; if I had given more in charity; if I had volunteered to help the homeless and the needy—maybe, just maybe God would have had mercy on him. Then, I'd think, maybe he wasn't dead; maybe he just physically disappeared, but his soul would live on. I could talk to his soul; I could ask him questions and wait desperately for answers. My heart bereaved. Was I insane? Was I feeble? Was I frightened by the unknown?

I kneeled.

God be with me!

God show me his face one more time!

God let me feel him!

God take away my pain and give me comfort!

God tell me he's fine!

God tell me that he's no longer worried about his children!

God tell me what I need to do to gain the strength I need to come to the realization that he is truly gone and that nothing I say or do will change the echoes of my crying heart.

Before a loss, it seems like you will do anything if only your loved one would be spared . . . We want to go back in time: find the tumor sooner, recognize the illness more quickly, stop the accident from happening . . . if only, if only, if only.

—David Kessler and Elizabeth Kubler Ross
On Grief and Grieving, 2005

Chapter 17

Rituals and Defiance

Disoriented, I looked around Mazen's living room after our trip to the funeral home. "What time is it?"

"You fell asleep. We didn't want to disturb you," my mother said. "You should go home, take a shower, and get some sleep. You need to be at the mosque by 8:30 for the service."

The Mosque? The service? I wish Muslims didn't have to bury the dead immediately. I needed time to absorb the fact that Mazen was no longer among us. I was shattered by her words. I wailed and cried as I walked toward the door, pressing my hand against my chest to suppress the pain emanating from the puncture of this wound. I held onto the wall, feeling nauseous and disoriented. Mazen's son Mahmoud ran toward me and said, "*Tata*, please don't go. Please sleep with us tonight. Baba's not here anymore."

I tried to make sense of what he'd said. I wondered how Mazen, helpless and bedridden, had been able to color the life of his son with a deep sense of security and now that it was gone, how this little four-year-old yearned for his father's replacement. He yearned for love and comfort. He may not have known much about death, but his level of belief was archetypal or somehow instinctively embedded in his subconscious mind. It was the kind of instinctive knowledge that Noam Chomsky described in his analysis of children's innate ability to conjugate verbs from their present to their past tenses without knowing the grammar rules associated with them. Mahmoud was definitely too young to make logic from the situation, but wise enough to know that his paternal grandmother was next in line to his father. His words struck a deep note.

I hugged him, held his shoulders back, and looked into his sad eyes. "I'm very tired and I need to rest."

He ran to his mother.

It broke my heart to walk away from his saddened face, but I had no alternative. I was vacillating between the world of the living and the world of the dead, and I feared that my presence at that very moment would do him more harm than good.

My sister Samerah, who stood nearby, was taken aback by the conversation and moved her head to and fro. She took hold of my arm and offered to drive me home. I accepted her offer knowing that I was in no condition to drive alone, especially at night. Her face had softened with age, but her eyes were moist. She reached out for a cigarette, placed it between her lips, and said nothing. She loved Mazen so much that it was difficult for her to listen and hold back from fighting her own anger as she removed her unlit cigarette and uttered, "He was a fun and loving nephew, and I am going to miss him." We both cried.

I pleaded with God to alleviate my pain and to help me understand the meaning behind life and death. Part of my own being had been torn away, and my wound was bleeding profusely.

I stuttered as I repeated my mother's words, *"prepare yourself,"* and wondered how she presumed that burying my son was something I could prepare for. There is no preparation or final settlement with death. Death has no resolution. I could never look it in the face and say, "We can now develop a friendship." To arrive at a peace treaty with death is like sailing across the oceans and never reaching a destination.

In fact, the final image of Mazen's pale face continued to flash in my memory, and might carry on until I am rescued by death itself.

A chilly morning. Rummaging through my clothes to find something black, formal, and warm, I screamed, "Mazen! No! I am not going to find something to wear for your funeral. Who's going to give you your Roxinal, Dilantin, Decadron, and your Ativan? Who's going to make you feel better? Oh no, you're not gone! You're still with me! Mazen...please tell me where you are. Please answer me! Each day you lived was a blessing!"

I wasn't sure my black sweater and polyester pants were going to shield me from the piercing wind of the cemetery.

I dropped to the floor and plunged into a world where the song of hope had faded, leaving me helpless. Ernie watched me. He raised me to my feet and said, "Come on, Honey! Here, put this on and let's go." I took the black pantsuit, tripped a few times as I put it on, and dragged myself toward the door. He wrapped a black wool shawl over my shoulders, drew me toward him, gave me a tight hug, and whispered, "Mazen is resting. He is no longer suffering."

"How do you know he was suffering? He wasn't able to communicate. How do you know he's resting? Has anyone ever returned to let us know? If he was in pain, is there a theologian or philosopher who has confirmed suffering ends with death?"

He stared at me with an unarticulated silence that made me wonder if he knew more than I did. I felt defeated.

I thought repeatedly to myself...*There are thousands of complex and erudite answers, but in the end, none satisfied me. Not one has rationalized the concept of life and death. Is there life after death? Is there such a thing as purgatory? Is Mazen's soul resting among us or is it traveling between the universe and the heavens? I will never know.*

In silence, we drove to the mosque at 8:30 a.m. Mazen's body was scheduled to arrive from the funeral home by 9:00 a.m. As we approached the front entrance, I observed the sad faces of the crowds of young men and women waiting for the arrival of the hearse. They stood at the footsteps of the mosque's main entrance. I wondered if rising from their beds on an early Saturday morning was an affirmation of Mazen's lovable and illuminating character or a sign of their own fears and compulsions in connecting with death. Death manifests itself in our lives no matter how beautiful. Once we realize that a close friend no longer exists, it is difficult to eradicate his or her memory and even more difficult to suspend the thought that we, too, will one day fall into the abyss of the underworld.

Ernie dropped me off at the rear entrance where I wouldn't have to face or talk to people. I didn't want the grief taking over my life to rise to the surface and add to my bereavement. I entered the mosque staring at the ground until I reached the lecture hall. I followed tradition and sat quietly in the front row. A few minutes later, I heard loud cries. I looked back only to see Rania and Dania sharing their grief with relatives and close friends. They walked toward me in a daze as though they were still sorting things out, wondering why they were even at the mosque. They moved with caution between the rows of chairs to sit next to me. Mona was sitting a few chairs down from me. She cried and moved her hands across her lap as though she had some unfinished business and yearned for Mazen's return to help her. She was mourning alongside her mother and sisters who tried hard to buffer against her loneliness. Their hands caressed her hair, and then slid gently to her arm as her head rested on her mother's shoulder.

Family and friends charged in from all over the city. Many of Mazen's relatives who lived out of state and overseas were scheduled to arrive before the burial. In the throes of my grief, seeing the friends and relatives that he had known and played with since childhood briefly lifted the cloud of gloom that had hung over my head all morning. The lecture hall became crowded and the overflow of people was directed to the banquet hall.

I prayed that time would come to a standstill; not wanting to believe it was Mazen's funeral. Suddenly, a cold draft filled the room. A strange aroma trickled up my nose. *Was this the scent of his soul?* The air seemed permeated with an unbearable affliction, especially upon hearing the sudden commotion, the men's loud shouts of *"Allahu Akbar,"* "God is great."

I leaned back on my chair, gasping for breath. The casket had arrived. It felt as if my trachea had swollen shut. My daughters watched me gasp for breath. Panicking, they pulled me from my chair and stretched my arms outward until I was finally able to breathe.

I thought of the time their father died and how, as young, heartbroken teenagers, they held onto me as we walked behind the procession. I worried about them and the pain they were experiencing after losing their father, their brother, and now their fear of losing me. Rania sat close to me and said, "Mama, it's kind of like a habitual impulse. I vowed never to take the lives of my loved ones for granted. I want you to know that after the death of my father and brother, you are my only connection to this world. I want to protect you. I fear for you."

Family, friends, and relatives carried Mazen's casket to the lecture hall. They placed it against the wall, facing the row of chairs where I was sitting. For a brief moment, I froze and wondered if collectively, would it be possible for them to bring Mazen back to life? *Was I hallucinating or insane? Were my thoughts violating social norms? Was I questioning the actions of the Omnipotent?*

If I questioned God's actions, I might lessen my chances of going to Heaven or even seeing Mazen after my death. I dismissed my paranoia. Mazen was on his way to heaven after having endured not so much the physical pain, but the mental agony of leaving his wife and young children behind.

I wanted to keep peace with God. I wanted to be with Mazen. I straightened up and walked toward the casket as though to greet him. I put my chair by the casket and hoped the Imam wouldn't object.

After making sure Mazen's head was positioned toward the east or perpendicular to the *Qibla*, the House of God located in Mecca, Saudi Arabia, the funeral home director opened the upper half of the casket and covered it with a loosely woven nylon veil. He was directed by the Imam to use a veil in all cases of open caskets (some Muslims do not have open caskets) to prevent their loved ones from touching the deceased. Once the deceased is washed and prayed over, he or she should no longer be touched by the living.

I hovered over his pale face, framed by the contours of his white *kafan.* He looked angelic and serene. Every now and then, I'd lower my head toward his face with the urge to kiss his cheek. Finally, and with hope that God would be compassionate and understanding, I kissed his forehead as I did when he was a newborn. I wanted to let him know that I was still watching over him. After several repetitions, I felt as though he was alive again. Without hesitation, this time, I lifted the veil and placed my warm lips against his cold cheeks. These lasted on and off for an hour or until the eulogies were over.

The Imam, who had been silently observing my actions, arose from his seat and walked toward me. He whispered, "No, *Um Mazen* (mother of Mazen, the traditional Arab name that a mother is given after the birth of her first-born son) please, do not touch him. His body has been washed and purified and what you are doing will require that he be washed again. Please stop."

I challenged his request. "I am his mother and he is part of me. Pressing my lips against his face and forehead is my way of connecting spiritually with him."

He stood frozen for a while then said, "Well, I guess it doesn't matter now, it's time to carry him to his final destination."

He directed the men to take the casket to the prayer room to finalize the service.

I moved to the side as I watched them carry Mazen to the prayer room where they would perform *salat al janazah,* a prayer to seek pardon for the deceased before the burial.

I followed them knowing I was in no state to make close and intense connections with the Imam's prayers. I stood near the entrance of the prayer room to observe Mazen's dark, russet coffin sway back and forth over the shoulders of his uncles, cousins, and friends as they repeatedly cried, *"La illaha Ila Allah"* or *"there is no god but God"* an Islamic phrase called *Shahada.* The *Shahada* is the Muslim's declaration of the belief in the oneness of God. By pausing every thirty seconds while struggling to carry the coffin upright, they were repeating the phrase loud enough to echo across the prayer room to confirm Mazen's devotion to the belief in the oneness of God. By publically endorsing Mazen's belief in this concept, they hoped to secure his residence in heaven.

My feet ventured a few steps into the inky darkness and stopped. I couldn't move. I wasn't ready for the adieu. It was too soon. Mazen's death cut short the chronological flow of human relationships and I knew at that moment I would never be ready and my grief would never be over. I longed for the Imam's final prayers to suppress my memories of the horrifying moments following Mazen's initial diagnosis, but the prayers compelled me to relive them.

I feared the trip to the cemetery. I knew once Mazen's casket was lowered into the ground, my battle to keep him close by would be over and God's mission would be accomplished. I thought of my defeat and helplessness. I wondered why God helped me jump through the hoops over the years to protect Mazen from numerous and unfathomable situations, yet today, He let me down. I yearned for justification and acceptance.

Mazen's death took me away from the active stream of life and the hours ahead were like unknown visitors invading my world.

Mazen's cancer diagnosis stirred me in the wrong direction. I submerged myself in darkness and kept asking, "Why him and not me?" Before his death, my sister told me to see my doctor. I asked her, "Why? I'm not sick! Mazen is!" But I knew something was wrong with me. I felt weak and depressed. Once in the doctor's office, I couldn't stop crying. He convinced me to take Prozac. I reached out for my first pill as I questioned the natural order of existentialism and sobbed. Twenty minutes later, I felt *indifference.* It seemed as though nothing mattered anymore. My emotions were dry. My head no longer listened to my heart. I pulled the Prozac out of my medicine cabinet, stared at it intently, moved it around in my hands and tossed it in the trash. I swore that I would never take anything like it again. As long as Mazen was alive, I preferred to put up a strong front, keep a happy face, and try not to let him think that he was not going to win the battle. I also wanted to be alert and ready if and when Mazen's doctors asked for my opinion on medical treatments and procedures. But after his death, my body ached. My sighs were prolonged moments of agony. My eyes burned. The air howled around me. I came to the realization that something was terribly wrong and that perhaps an anti-depressant would conceal the darkness that lived in side of me and lift me from the vaults of my trembling spirit. If I didn't, I feared I'd be miserable and make the lives of those around me extremely unpleasant. I needed to adapt to my surroundings. I needed something, at least short-term or until I was strong enough to overcome the adversities of my existence. My psychological well-being became crucial. I took Wellbutrin for three years.

> After bargaining, our attention moves squarely into the present. . .
> It's important to understand that this depression is not a sign of
> mental illness. It is the appropriate response to a great loss.
>
> —David Kessler and Elizabeth Kubler Ross
> *On Grief and Grieving,* 2005

Chapter 18

The Green Tent

The *salat al janazah* or the funeral prayer at the mosque was over, and it was time to carry Mazen to the cemetery. Melancholy at heart; I wasn't sure what to do. I felt as though dragged into the wilderness to intermingle with the sphere of death. My husband, who noticed me wandering off, took my hand to walk me to the car. I was frightened of what lay ahead and angry at the world and the concept of human bondage to God and the meaning behind life and death. I struggled with the interpretations of Scripture and my relationship with God. I didn't want to be held captive to a power beyond my control unless I knew my obedience to that power would lead to righteousness, and righteousness would eventually lead me to my son.

Despite all, my belief in God and the afterlife gave me something to look forward to. I hoped I would see Mazen again, but, despite this faith, I felt like a truth seeker in a dark forest. *What is the truth behind life and death, and where did Mazen go?* These were questions that I wanted answers to, and I didn't feel I was close to finding them. To take the blame away from God, I compelled myself to believe that some mortal was at fault, but I didn't know at whom I wanted to shake an accusing finger.

I walked ahead of Ernie and pulled his hand to move quickly toward the back exit of the mosque while staring at the ground. The crowd thickened as everyone tried to exit at once. Lifting my eyes reluctantly as I approached the lobby, I noticed the dispirited faces of friends and family members standing near the door. Grief weighed heavy in the atmosphere as they stood around me to share in my sorrow. I looked at my friend Lois, who waited for me near the exit.

"I'm embarking on a spiritual journey to the underworld. I'm scared," I said.

She pressed my arm gently with her fingers as if to say, *I love you and I'm hurting with you*, while other female friends drew me closer to them to whisper words of comfort. Each time, I managed to say "thank you," my lips trembled and my heart skipped. The faint smell of dust and human flesh filled my nostrils with the odor of death. I took a few deep breaths and prayed I would make it to the car without fainting. Ernie held onto my arm to make sure I didn't fall. My legs quivered as I inched my way through the parking lot to the car. I yearned to connect with Mazen's spirit. The reflection of his soul surrounded me as I began to face the painful reality of his passing. I had adhered to the spiritual since my struggle against the most horrendous odds left me vulnerable. At that moment, I felt weak. My faith in God and my spirituality were my only source of comfort.

Mazen had died on Good Friday and a week later, my friend Diane offered me a *pieta* made of soft white plaster. "Mary, I hope I'm not offending you, but I want you to have this. As a Catholic, I believe this will bring you comfort. Mazen's death was so coincidental with that of Jesus that I thought this might be appropriate. Jesus was thirty-three, he suffered, his mother's name was Mary, and he died on Good Friday."

I took it from her hand and gently rolled my fingertips across the Virgin Mary's face and along the length of Jesus's body with hope that Mazen would reappear to me as Jesus had presumably reappeared to his mother. Yet I knew that my wound was too fresh and such thoughts were mere fantasies. They had no truth in a world where miracles were reserved for prophets. My only hope was that Mazen would reappear to me in my dreams and transform my nocturnal world of darkness into one of light. I yearned to see his innocent face like the day I took him in my arms for the first time. His eyes bore the blind cry of infancy and grew sweeter over the years as they filled with endless words of silent conversations. I raised my eyes at the time toward the skies and spoke softly to God . . . *He's with you now . . . Please take care of him . . . He's at your mercy . . .*

Belief in God and the afterlife was a kind of urge to dwell in the world of the spirit. It was a world free of barriers. It gave me a lift to take away the structure of the universe, leaving me bare and numb to the cries of my soul. My feelings were tantamount to an admission that I wanted to die, but I somehow knew that God wasn't ready for me. Conventional medicine had betrayed me, and the hurt that resulted as an inevitable discrepancy between my expectations and reality was unbearable. I wanted to transform my pain to divine nourishment through prayer and hope of a reunion, but the mental agony resulting from my loss was obstructing my thinking.

It was a chilly morning. I shivered. Near my car, the heat from the warm hand of a colleague penetrated through my skin and made its way to my tingling blood vessels. Impacted by my posture, I wasn't sure whether the tingling was caused by post-polio syndrome or pressure on the nerves of my spine. All I knew is that I couldn't pull myself up straight. I stood frozen. My legs trembled, intensely numb and unpredictable.

I remember my sister-in-law Asyah had bent at the waist after her son was killed in a car accident in Washington D.C. many years back. For a moment, I'd thought she'd aged twenty years as I watched her creep along the length of her thirty-three- year-old son's coffin. She held onto its edges as though her son was an infant and she feared he was going to fall off the edge of his bed. A few seconds later, she ran across the funeral home display room screaming and pleading with God to return her son to her. Her supplications, "God . . .please send him back to me long enough for me to say good-bye . . . I want to tell him how much he will be missed," sounded like faint echoes in the distance.

The slow-moving procession crept to the cemetery. The torment of my loss penetrated so deeply into my heart that I felt the pain would never come out again. My mother and father rode in the back seat with us. They clutched their Qurans and read prayers and supplications. Their words, as they raised and lowered the pitch of their voices to comply with the lexical and grammatical tone variations of standard Arabic, echoed in my ears with a peculiar severity. What had always sounded like a rhythmic delight transformed into heavy moans and mortal cries. It made me wonder if, within the sphere of religious theory, scripture was intended to keep Mazen in remembrance or to confirm the painful reality of his passing. Occasionally, the mourners sighed deeply and lifted their eyes from the fine print of the Quran to question who might be in the car ahead of us. I, in turn, spent what seemed like lifeless moments wishing there was some potion I could drink to make my pain disappear.

I shuddered each time I thought of Mazen's death and vowed to keep silent throughout the commute as my anger began to rise against my utter exhaustion and confusion. The fog began to dissipate from the windshield and the weight of my burden accompanied by my mute fear of the burial process gave way to the sunlight that nestled in my eyes. I fumbled through my purse to find my sunglasses with hope that they would shade my eyes from the striking sunrays. Weeds grew beside the dark waters alongside the road and the wildflowers of the sun-stricken earth behind them were ready to sprout. I assumed that life would pull me along whether I gave it my blessing or not. Many mourners before me had lived like caterpillars and emerged from a world surrounded by darkness into triumphant butterflies. I wondered how I would ever overcome Mazen's death.

When we approached the cemetery, my mother began to wail. She ran toward the designated location of Mazen's grave by an open green tent and graveside chairs and equipment. My father rushed out of the car to join my brothers, who were standing at a distance, waiting for the hearse to arrive. Family and friends arrived and gathered around the green tent. At first, the image of their dark figures was so glossy that they reflected the sunshine with a gleam, but as they began to multiply, their black clothing turned the green landscape into mosaic shades of gray earth. While observing the display of rituals, the men prepared to greet the coffin, and the women visited surrounding gravesites of friends and family members to read the *Fatha,* the opening chapter of the Quran and the most cited of all Quranic verses.

I massaged my legs to reduce the muscle and joint weakness. I aligned them next to each other, sprang out of the car, and landed on the damp grass. I stood frozen next to Ernie, who stood against the car waiting for me to join him. I didn't want to look at people, nor did I want to approach the green tent. I looked down at the ground and wept. I was afraid. I didn't know what to expect of myself or of others who were watching me. My body ached as I waited for the moment when Mazen's coffin arrived. I kept my distance, rested my head on Ernie's shoulder and prayed for Mazen's spirit to speak to me. I whispered to Ernie, "I am not going near that area. I don't want to watch Mazen's burial."

He nodded.

I had gone to the Memorial Garden Cemetery to attend burial services of friends and family members in the past, but, on this day, everything solid seemed fragmented, like stones crumbling from towers. The ground seemed uneven, almost moving. I wasn't sure if my state of despair had made me delusional or if the earth was literally eroding under my feet. I felt as if I were sinking and the ground rising above me. My daughter Dania walked toward me and took my hand for a split moment, then, yanked it away as though she had some unfinished business with her deceased brother, calling his name in a piercing scream. Her scream caused an emotional outburst from the elderly women standing near the tent. I wanted to carry Dania and flutter away, but my wings were broken. I wanted to at least hold her in my arms and tell her that everything was going to be fine, but I couldn't. I knew I'd be lying to her. I felt so paralyzed and incompetent. How could I tell anyone *I was fine?*

Once Dania's hysteria passed, Rania and Mona followed suit. By then, I sensed Mazen's spirit revolving around me like the sun reflecting from his coffin as he entered the cemetery over the shoulders of men who carried him to his final destination. As the men carried him to his gravesite, they stopped every ten steps to shout *"Allahu Akbar"* while everyone else waited patiently near the green tent standing above his grave.

The smell of freshly mown grass and loads of wreaths carried by friends and family members, who followed the coffin past the tombstones, gave me the courage to leave my station and visit Mazen's new home. It was a strenuous walk and the site would be my future home as well. Death is inevitable, so when the nurse had informed us that Mazen had only a few days to live, I asked Ernie to purchase three gravesites. He bought a bundle of four instead. I wanted to be buried next to Mazen. I wanted him on one side and Ernie on the other. I foresaw death as an alternate means to reunite with Mazen, and hoped that if the dead communicated with one another, proximity would make a difference.

I then froze in a windless space and imagined our new home filled with the fragrance and the fragile beauty of the wreaths and roses scattered around the tent, symbols of some sweet moral blossom telling the sorrow-stories of human mortality.

Ernie touched my shoulder. "Are you okay?"

I hate when I'm swept away by my daydreams and someone taps me on the shoulder to bring me back to the shaking voices of earth's creatures. When under stress, my mind becomes a rocky dwelling of peaceful yet deceptive moments. My rational mind is pushed into the furthest corner of my skull, replaced by the toxic paranoia of false assumptions. Observing the faces of the young and old around me led to feelings of guilt. I kept asking myself why Mazen's time came before mine. I had no answer. I became restless and cold. I didn't know whether to stay outside or to sit in the car. I yearned for God to teach me the art of handling death and how to return life to my dead soul. I preferred death to life, but I couldn't spend time worrying about when I was going to die. I just wanted to make it through the days and years ahead to be prepared for a reunion.

I stood silently, watching the preparations for Mazen's burial as though floating between two mountains, only to see Mazen's coffin sink into oblivion and me with him. I hoped that his sinking corpse would convert into energy, and that Mazen's lifeless mass would come back to this existence. Instead, energy surged through my body, and I heard myself screaming as though I was under attack by the big black snake of my old dream, the snake that had initiated the onset of this dreadful tragedy twenty months earlier.

My cries stimulated louder cries from my daughters and even though it took forty minutes to drive back home, it felt as though seconds later, I lay in bed, holding onto the Quran and begging God for spiritual relief.

When people told me that the world was going to be sweet again, I wondered if that could ever be possible. All I knew was that my life had been shattered. After years of living through denial, anger, bargaining, and depression, I knew I had to change. I taught my mind, heart, and body to assimilate the events of my everyday life even though I never stopped thinking of Mazen. I continued to hear his voice and feel his gentle spirit, but I learned to remove all of the negatives from my life so that I might grow stronger. As a result, the hungry beast of death stopped roaring in my head. Mazen was with me in heart and soul. He'd become part of me. I found rest.

Chapter 19

A Higher Plateau

All afternoon Mazen's house filled with the shadows of people dressed in black. A Middle Eastern tradition to greet guests after the death of a loved one, this reception takes place for seven days in the deceased's home or the home of a close relative. Most friends and relatives take time from their busy schedules to pay their respects.

My heart was melting. Oblivious to friends and family, I feared the future without Mazen. I wanted to run outside, scream, and raise my arms in the air to draw the clouds closer to me with the hope of finding a way to reach him. I loved Rania, Dania, Adam, and my husband, but without Mazen, I felt as though I'd be forever alone.

"Calm down, sweetheart," Mom said, rocking me in her arms.

I wished the world were deathless. I meditated for a pulsing moment, stood up, fumbled though my purse to find my car keys, and walked out, ignoring the inquisitive faces of friends and family. I stood on the porch for a second, slouching, then followed my feet as they led me down the stairs and toward the street. I glanced up for a split-second at Mazen's car parked in front of his home. I ran my hand across the side door, thinking of the secrets of love, life, and death, wiped my tears with the back of my hand, and climbed into my bronze Windstar. I turned on the ignition and without thinking, drove to a park a few blocks away from Mazen's home. I wanted to be alone so that I could let out wails of self-pity. I felt squeezed between the world of the living and the world of the dead. I tried to think, but my brain was as numb as my body.

When I raised my head to question God, I saw Mazen's image. He looked down at me with a sacredness of heart. I felt a troubled joy as I slouched in my seat. Mazen looked healthy, as he had before his radiation and treatments, but he seemed resigned.

Feeling disconnected, I said in a soft tone, "Mazen, it's so nice to see you. I'm coming. I don't know how, but I'll be joining you soon. I know I will."

Then, the unthinkable happened. He frowned and jerked his head sideways as though angry with me. He said, "No, you're not! You need to stay where you are. You need to take care of my children. You need to watch over them!"

I leaned my head on the steering wheel. *I thought he'd be happy to know I would join him. I wanted to be part of his world. I wanted my resentment of walking among the living to go away.*

For an awful moment, I felt felled by an unpredictable bullet or shrapnel. I looked up to gaze at Mazen...he was gone.

A rush of cold blood ran through my body. I shivered and tried to absorb what had happened and wondered if I had become delusional. I drove back to Mazen's home.

Rania looked at me. "Are you all right? Where did you go?"

"Nowhere," I said, hoping she wouldn't ask again.

Confused, she walked away.

I wasn't able to dismiss readily what had happened. It wasn't until months later in a lengthy conversation with my uncle that I learned the two children he lost had looked down at him from the sky to signal that their immortal souls would forever visit him. I shared my story and he convinced me I wasn't fantasizing. He smiled empathetically. "Sometimes, our loved ones communicate with us through visualization and silent speech."

After hearing his words, my relationship with God was lifted to a higher plateau. I believed, as did my uncle, that this was a tinge of devotion and that God adorns our pain in mysterious ways.

But in the meantime, the difficulty of accepting Mazen's death consumed us all. Mona, sitting with her face buried in her hands, fell into long periods of silence. She was unable to focus on anyone except her two year-old son Jemail, when he demanded her attention. Even then, she'd look at her sisters and mumble with a flat voice, "Will one of you please take him?"

I leaned motionless against a wall and thought of Mazen's father and the day I'd learned he had terminal cancer.

We cannot afford to forget any experience, not even the most painful.

—Dag Hammarskjold

Chapter 20

The Hidden Truth

Once the reception week was over, I wasn't sure how to accept the unspeakable torment of Mazen's death and still live productively. My heart lost its regular and healthy throb, leaving me powerless and weak as I dragged my heavy feet around the house. I wandered blindly into the dark labyrinth of sacred texts and volumes of self-help books sworn by reviewers to cast light on those who were on the verge of lunacy. I hoped to remain sane and to climb to some point of understanding. I still yearned to know the location of Mazen's soul. I still felt desperate to take root in his world and connect with him physically or in my dreams rather than feel like a captured slave pleading for mercy. I wasn't sure if I followed the footsteps of grievers by listening to their stories, prayed more frequently, made amends with God, went on pilgrimage, or complied with the five pillars of Islam that I would learn the truth hiding with God behind the silence of eternity. I could only hope to find some form of truth, some form of reason.

Sinking into the abyss of my heart, I continued to search for answers. I needed to fill the emptiness of my soul with enlightenment and knowledge. I felt Mazen's spirit wrap itself around me to fill the void, yet it left me with a strange fear of the afterlife and its mysteries. My hopes to connect with his soul were crucified. I did not hear the tune of Mazen's singing spirit, nor was I able to gaze at its beauty, or smell its perfume like several clergy, claiming to be knowledgeable, had promised. Life was still. I writhed with pain, convulsions of pain, and loathed the moral agony of speaking to myself throughout the day, hoping to find answers to Mazen's whereabouts. Thinking of him with God gave me comfort, but my eyes were veiled to God's truth of where Mazen's soul might be. I felt persecuted for a crime I did not commit. *Why was the truth of his whereabouts so obscure?*

My eyes pleaded for someone to draw the blinds away from the windows and shed light on the mystery of his location and on my ignorance. Nothing I read or understood from the Quran, the Bible, or heard from clergymen satisfied my need to know. It was like reading my way through a maze only to find myself even more lost. I felt helpless and defeated. *Was I wrong? Was Mazen not with God? If not, where was he? Did his soul die with him? It couldn't have. The Quran states that the soul never dies. Then why can't I find the truth?* I prayed that Mazen was dwelling in purgatory, at least, until he reached his final abode. I stretched my arms daily to the skies and lifted my eyes heavenward uttering supplications and prayers that would lead me to the majestic understanding of God's truth.

I missed Mazen. Each night before I went to sleep, I craved a visitation, but my dreams were dismantling my memories of him and causing me more grief. I never found the strength to embrace him while he was ill and to say to him, "We will always be together." I feared that showing my sadness would cause him fear and harm him further or subtract from the already perishing energy that had circulated between us. I yearned to hold him against my bosom and tell him how much I loved him, but dreaded that my actions would speak alongside the burning flames of his predicted destiny and that would scare him. I refrained.

I lived in anticipation that there might be a reunion between us in the afterlife and that Mazen would have a second chance to see his family members and cuddle with his wife and children. Mazen and his family were like flowers that bloomed year-round, spreading their loving fragrance around their home and adding to the richness of my own life by observing their happiness. Mazen's children were the garment of his heritage and the breath that gave him life.

When his neurologist had run out of treatments, he had stood up from behind his desk, walked toward Mazen, took his hand and said, "I'm sorry, but there is nothing else I can do..." Mazen, squirming in his seat, looked up at him. "What about my children?" he retorted with a flush of pain swooping over his brow.

With a slow, pitiful gesture, the doctor put his hand on Mazen's head. "I'm so sorry..." Then he stood stranded in his own silence.

This scene would flash through my mind and would forever flare against the immediate darkness of my world.

My wounds were beginning to destroy what was left of my spirit and to drag me into a world of ignorance and cruelty. I'd become bitter. My voice filled with loathing and contempt toward whomever stood in my way, innocent or guilty. I didn't know what was happening to me. As I searched for the truth, I found myself rebelling against the false claims of the learned or those who claimed to know the whereabouts of the soul. They were like thieves who stole the light of my soul to replace it with a forest of thick branches and darkness. I changed. I broke the chain of my previously harmonious character and became unhappy and wretched. I hated myself. I hated life. I didn't have any serious qualms about doing things right or caring about what others might think. I built an alien framework around my body to protect me from the shocking and unsympathetic words of those who believed I needed to move forward.

The laceration in my heart was invisible to the common eye. I wondered if my pain would follow me to the grave or if it would develop a kind of intimacy between heaven and Earth that would ultimately bring forth the cradle of my understanding. I wanted to hear the echo of God's comforting words so that I might be relieved. Day after day, I wanted to die.

A few weeks after Mazen's death, I lifted my eyes to the clouds and said, *"Come now, wicked death. Tell me that I am going to meet again with Mazen. Don't lead me astray and cause me to vanish in a crumbling world of misconceptions. If I must battle with you to understand the truth, then I am armed and ready. Please, carve my path with the beauty of understanding so that I can carry the weight of my heart and walk through life. I will rebuild my wings and lift myself to sip from the rim of God's blessings as the infant would suck from its mother's nipples to feel satisfied and complete. Please tell me the truth. Soothe me and tell me that we will be reunited."*

Over time, Mazen's death became my soul keeper. It kept me alive and helped me learn from the ever-recurring agony that life after losing him could be destructive only if I allowed it to be. I knew I must embrace my existence and take charge of my future because if I didn't, I might fall into a blacker depth of haunting moments brooding in my mind from the day Mazen was diagnosed. There were times when people would say to me—*"How do you do it? How can you lose a child and yet continue to live a normal life? Do you have a secret?"* and my response was always, *"How do you know how I feel and what choice do I have, anyway?"*

Their words would leave my heart lonely and cold. I could but tremble in the face of such cruel inquisitions, and prayed that the simple bliss of understanding would cross their hearts and feed their need for enlightenment in such matters. Countless mothers and fathers die shortly after burying their children, and I wonder if they lost their lives as a direct consequence of their children's deaths or a state of being that kept them from searching for the truth. They might have been too fixated on "death" itself and lost their belief in Scriptural Authority, the afterlife, and the promise of a reunion.

My family was kind and supportive, but I sensed the need to return to work. I returned a week after Mazen's burial to conceal my emotions from my loved ones. They constantly called to check on me, but after listening on a daily basis to the sweetness of their words and the pity kneaded with their compassion, I felt like I was stamped with damnation. I needed to separate myself from their golden voices and connect with the eyes of my colleagues and students who, for a change, would help present life as less holy and more factual. I didn't want to be perceived as a sacred image of sinless motherhood that should drink sacred oils and wine in order to bury the pain that seemed to have a noble art of its own. The pain took pride in cutting razor deep into the holy impulses of my heart to remind me of Mazen's death at every moment of the day, and my only outlet was work. I was like the Greek goddess Persephone returning to the upper world to give birth to the seeds of vegetation.

Then, Truth unveiled itself to me. I found myself standing in an imaginary garden without walls contemplating the truth. Even though the world can sometimes be hostile, I had no reason to believe that I wasn't going to reunite with Mazen. I'd frequently go stooping away along the earth, plucking stories from the tales of the imams, priests, and rabbis who flirted imaginatively with their own beliefs that added negative weight to the mysteries that already overburdened my heart. They said that over time I would understand God's reason for taking Mazen. I didn't know whether to believe them or not, but again, it was better to believe in the stories of my forefathers than to adopt the belief that the mystical reality of the "soul" didn't exist.

At times, when reason failed me, I huddled around the warmth of the parapsychological stories of people and their experiences with the secrets of life and death. Their stories defied reason, but I believed them because I was beginning to have experiences that I will share with readers in the epilogue. My conscious and subconscious minds were collecting energy from each other. I wanted them to integrate and to give me peace.

As strange as this may seem, I began to see, feel, and hear Mazen, consciously and subconsciously, and it was a few months later that I felt his energy penetrate my body and become an integral part of me. If someone mentioned his name, I would smile instead of crying and if the high tide of my feelings could speak, it would reveal that love and flesh can become one, like the fetus and its mother when they share nutrient-rich blood.

I was finally satisfied, at least, temporarily. True, we are born to die, but some of us deny the ailment of death with all its afflictions and hope it will only reach the old and evil. We are all capable of seeking eternal joy or sorrow, but it is how we perceive the truth of where we might be when we die that makes a difference in how we accept or despise death. I was compelled to accept it. My injured wings began to take flight.

I came to the realization that the world was nothing but a temporary passage, a passage to an eternal life, a life that would ultimately reunite me with Mazen. My heart was wounded and my spirit was saddened and nothing could change that, but I'd come to grips with the reality that humans are powerless and fate can never be controlled. As Gibran Khalil Gibran wrote in his collected works, "Life was given in marriage to death," and one cannot exist without the other. No one knows when or how we will be carried to our tombs, but we know for certain that no one is deathless. The healing process may differ from person to person, but in the end, we learn to accept what we thought we'd never be able to accept. We can't purchase relief; it is given to us over time. We must accept our misfortune. We must lift ourselves from the torment and decaying ruins of death's aftermath and learn to live in the warmth of our loved one's spirit. Our hearts and minds work together to give us the power we need to make sense of a senseless loss and feel safe in the shadows of a stolen life. I have found the power to feel Mazen's existence and to infinitely cherish his memories.

> Acceptance is . . . about accepting the reality that our loved one is physically gone and recognizing that this new reality is the permanent reality. . .We begin to live again, but we cannot do so until we have given grief its time.
>
> —David Kessler and Elizabeth Kubler Ross
> *On Grief and Grieving,* 2005

Epilogue

Many springs have come and gone and much of my pain has settled in the midst of a new Earth garmented with colorful daisies and roses, and the smile of sunset. The sun's rays cast their shadows across the glossy granite and rectangular slabs that wrap their heavy arms around our peacefully resting children. They are now in a place that is neither part of this world nor part of the afterlife. To lighten my burden, I find solace in joining groups of mourning mothers and fathers who are strangers yet not strangers, to greet each other at the cemetery to baptize our hearts in the pools of our tears. We hold each other's hands to laugh and reminisce about our children. We turn the earth into spring gardens and walk along the edges of our children's crumbled temples, knowing that those judging our spirits will testify to our pain, a pain that never seems to perish.

During our visits, we talk about our children and praise their triumphs in board games or childhood wars with toy tanks and GI Joes, and mourn our deceptions in their battles with cancer or sudden loss of life. Our sun-warmed conversations eventually turn into screams that sweep our private world with roaring cries and voices that resonate through the corridors of time, as if we are thrown into a flaming fire, repeatedly. Our choked hearts pump muffled tempests that run through our veins to strike our spirits with occasional outbursts of scattered emotions and burning tears. Moreover, after years of reaching out and sharing in each other's grief, I have learned the art of balancing my emotions. I have learned to fulfill myself more completely and directly with the sighing breath of death.

The occasional and unpredictable emotional outbursts, whether in the company of mourners or alone, have assisted in rebalancing my life and have given me the strength I need to be productive in my day-to-day activities. The increase in dopamine released by emotional outbursts, along with the fluttering in my stomach, sanctifies me with spiritual wisdom and the notion that God must have His reasons to lay His heavy hand on me and to drive my soul to a shambles. Because loneliness was born with Mazen's death, and with loneliness was born a strong desire to search for God's reasoning and to find inner solace. Fortunately, and not long after Mazen's death, I found both in the breast of His silence.

God showed His mercy the night Mazen came to me in my dream, several months after he had passed. Before my dream, my pain travelled in unison throughout my body, making me wonder if life was worth living without my firstborn, my best friend. From the day Mazen was old enough to walk, he listened to me cry and wiped away my tears with his tiny fingers. He gave me hope when I was in despair and laughter when I was in tears. As an adult, and among the many sports that we practiced to entertain each other, he enjoyed listening to my amateur interpretations of his dreams. He once rushed over about a month before he was given a terminal diagnosis with his hand clasped onto his heart and said, "Mama, I had a very rich and compelling dream, but I woke up feeling sad. I saw myself sitting at the top of a mountain looking down at the beauty of the Earth, and then, it felt like someone was choking me, and I woke up. What does this mean?"

Smiling, I replied, "Remember our French neighbor in Lebanon, Madame Bouchet?

"Yes, I remember her."

"Do you remember that she believed she had once been a queen and was reincarnated as an ordinary citizen? Well, I think your dream is revealing that you're like her. You were once a king, except you will fall and be reincarnated as a prince. Either way, it's good..."

I lied. The dream disturbed me, but I hid my fears and laughed about people whose lives were consecrated unto their dreams and about how many interpretations lack credence. Research on the biopsychology of dreams is complex, and it will take more than the interpretations of a dream dictionary or the tales of the old to interpret the true meaning of a dream. There is no scientifically definitive interpretation of dreams, but certain theories have their own supporters, and I agree with the theory that dreams allow us to contextualize our emotions and give us the opportunity to work them out peacefully as we rest. Nightmares, unlike dreams, are a result of anxiety or outright fear, but they offer us the opportunity to heal some of the psychological imbalances that we deal with on a day-to-day basis or throughout the course of our lives. Mazen didn't say that he had had a nightmare, so I tried not to worry.

When I thought back on his dream toward the end of his life, I thought of the notion of *reincarnation*. My interpretations were accurate, except after being reincarnated into a prince, he struggled for twenty months to release himself from the shadows of a bubonic plague, and failed. Mazen's cancer was like a thief whose deepened greed swept away my most treasured possession, leaving me lost between the horizons of two worlds—the world of the dead and the world of the living.

At first, participating in the world of the dead gave me peace. It was a sort of peace that I could not experience by taking antidepressants or any other form of serotonin re-uptake inhibitors. I had a strong desire to separate myself from the real world and feel the touch of Mazen's invisible wings as he distanced himself from my reach, but then, we disconnected and Mazen began to fade away. Gravity was building the Earth and drawing me closer to the living and further from the dead. Mazen's spirit perched itself on the shoulders of angels that had once lifted me off my feet to dance around him and help me drift from the reality of his passing. The distance between us grew.

It is as if he were being transferred to a brilliant shade of light and I, to a prison cell of blinding darkness.

The obscure force that separated us dominated my spirit and confiscated my secret refuge. I am forced into seeing the concealed truth, a truth hidden behind the sunlight of the heavens. I have no place among the still shadows of the dead, and I sense that God has missioned me to return to the physical world though returning was painful. The Earth's crust roasted beneath my feet and penetrated through my ever-fading desire to stay alive. I had no choice but to meet pain with greater pain. To my troubled mind, dreams were sometimes comforting.

In the dream where God showed His mercy on me, Mazen was wearing his red polo shirt, a shirt that caused his deep black eyes to shine and reflect across the living room. He looked at me intently and said, "Mama...come here. I want you to sit next to me."

I was standing in the dining room about twenty feet away from him, dusting the table and moving the chairs around to avoid scratching the table's edges. I looked at him and said, "Can't you see I'm busy? Just say what you want. I can hear you."

"Mama, please come here," he said with a gentle smile. He patted the cushion next to him and signaled me to sit down. Whenever he was serious, he called me Mama instead of Mom.

I walked toward him. "It better be important."

As soon as I sat next to him, he hugged me tight and said, "I love you Mama..." and then, I woke.

My muscles ached. It felt as though Mazen's hug was real. Tears streamed down my cheeks, making me wonder if they were made of holy water. I beamed. If Sigmund Freud was right, and dreams are manifestations of our deepest anxieties and desires, then, my dream stands as evidence that my craving for a final hug and adieu from Mazen became a dream reality.

The healing process differs from person to person and the emotional pain and suffering that is experienced almost immediately after the loss of a loved one—a spouse, a child—leads to feelings of weakness and helplessness. After Mazen passed, I found myself removed from the physical world to become closely connected to the world of the mind, an area where grief took precedence over all else. I struggled to untangle my emotions from the tapestry of anger and resentment revolving through the asymmetric hemispheres of my brain in an effort to get closer to what made me angry so that I could try to balance things out. I searched for a balance between my positive and negative emotions in hope to reduce the rage I was experiencing and find relief. It was a struggle, but after acceptance of the unacceptable, I was able to find peace by releasing my emotions, letting go of my anger, and connecting with my inner strength.

Releasing emotions is often an intuitive reaction with the majority of people. Some scream, some moan quietly behind closed doors, while others live in denial from fear of what their emotions might trigger. Emotions, the interplay between one's thoughts and physical sensations can be valuable if we learn how to cope with them effectively. They reflect thought and thought leads to the evolution of the mind through use of the senses. Our senses allow us to become aware of our feelings as we hold our loved ones at the center of attention and take on the troublesome task of trying to make sense of our losses as I did when Mazen passed. When I feel troubled, my rational mind goes on "park mode," making it almost impossible for me to process information that might place me in touch with reality and the ever-changing rhythm of life. It's as if my body floats over the Earth and lands in the clouds for a moment of meditation. My psyche takes control of all that is happening and walks me through the evolutionary process without realizing that a profound change is paving its way through my subconscious. I know *now* my pain is not insurmountable, and as a friend told me when I lost my first husband many years ago, "Grief washes itself away like a bar of soap. Give it time and it will enter into the light of your subconscious to help you heal." I looked at her thinking, *how will this ever go away? A bar of soap? What amount of time is she talking about. . .days, months, years?*

My understanding of the dynamics of time became visible as I embarked on a "healing journey" after losing Mazen. I found that one element playing an important role in my transformation to acceptance was in fact, "time." Time, a key factor in the healing process and the conversion from pain to peace, is directly correlated to the many choices and decisions we make as we grieve. As much as I didn't think it mattered that I wasn't alone, I was relieved when I thought of how many parents had gone through this before me and how they, too, might be suffering from their loss.

An Italian woman asks, "Have you lived a good life?" and if the person says, "Yes," her reply is, "Then, you've never lost a child," and she is right. Once you lose a child, you lose part of you and your life will never be the same again, a reality that I strongly doubt any grieving parent would disagree with. The loss of Mazen made me feel vulnerable, as if someone had punctured a hole in my heart, leaving my right atrium intact so that I might continue to live. On the other hand, the slightest task made me feel like I was climbing out of a valley holding on to my heart rather than the earth beneath my feet. My heart would constantly shoot off sharp pain and the pain led it to beat faster, but strangely enough, it empowered me with a deep form of energy. This boost of energy drove me to dig into the depths of my soul and hold on to life like young fruit clinging on to the branch that gives it support. At times, however, this same energy would turn into burning thought and urge me to walk into places where there were no people. I was irritable and touchy. Not everyone knew what to say, especially people I barely knew, and those who considered themselves religious wizards assumed that if they quoted something from the Quran, Bible, or *Hadith*, I was supposed to say, "Yes, you're right. Now, I feel better." But I realized after Mazen's death that no one can tell us how to feel or walk beside us and say, "This is God's will." I would turn away thinking, this person may mean well, but she needs to educate her foolishness. Of course, it's God's will. It sure wasn't mine, but telling me, "It's God's will" does not take away my pain. It's like telling me, "When the sun goes down, it's night time." Logic is the last thing a grieving parent wants to deal with. I would rather someone say that Mazen has now risen to the stars by making up some form of fantasy so that I could freeze in the stillness of the night and watch his face glow across the universe.

We each deal with grief in our own way as both the internal forces within us and the external forces around us dictate the outcome of our reactions. In *A Broken Heart Still Beats* by Anne McCracken and Mary Semel, the poet James Russell Lowell is quoted after a friend talks to him about faith and immortality. Lowell had lost his second child and he wasn't prepared to submit his will to faith and immortality. He agreed with his friend, but he also stated:

> Immortal? I feel it and I know it,
> Who doubts it of such as she?
> But that is the Pang's very secret,
> Immortal away from me.

He is a believer, but he is stating a matter of fact. Yes, she's gone and there is an afterlife or a chance that he might see her again, but for the moment, she's no longer with him. And the same with Victor Hugo three years after his daughter died—his friends wanted him to go back to work. He wrote:

> Wan, pallid, livid, it may be,
> She asks, in her straight be and still,
> "Can father have forgotten me?
> No longer here?—I'm so chill."

For some of us, work is a distraction; at least it was for me. But for Victor Hugo and many others like him, work is the last place they want to be. He was afraid that his daughter might think that he'd forgotten all about her and that her *still* corpse would become too *chilly*. He wanted to offer her the warmth he had offered her while she was alive. To him, she was not a corpse. She was a person-body that needed warmth. None of us want to believe that our child will become cold and wither away as though they'd never existed. It takes time, months, sometimes years to learn how to replace what was once a beautiful, bundle of life with a *soul*.

The "soul" is all we have left. We carry our loved one's soul in our hearts and give it a new life. Just as God has given a new life to seeds that is seemingly dead, we resurrect our children into shapes and forms that offer us warmth and rest. I was under so much stress a week after Mazen died that I had no human form and my nothingness was prepared to find him even if I had to use my imagination. I drove to the park and prayed that no one would be there so that I could close my windows and scream. I thought of when I had locked myself in the car at the supermarket three weeks prior to Mazen's death, sealed the windows, and cried, as I pitied my limitations of trying to keep Mazen alive. Shortly after, a police officer tapped at my window and told me to go home. Thinking of the same situation while at the park, I scouted the area before I allowed myself to wail. My wailing became so intense that the windshield fogged up as my eyes followed the invisible life trail that led them toward the sky. Mazen's face and upper torso appeared to me. This is a miracle, I thought, as I sat up straight, wiped my tears with the back of my hand and whispered to him. After he disagreed with my desire to be with him, telling me he needed me to look after his children, he disappeared like the flame of a candlelight blown away by a thousand breaths. I was shaken by the experience. It wasn't until later that I asked friends and relatives who had lost their children if they'd ever had a similar experience, and they would smile. Their smiles were answers to an impending truth, a truth that made the most logical person surrender to a world of peace that goes beyond all understanding. Whether it was a coincidence, a random hallucination, or an actual intervention on behalf of my subconscious, I really don't know, but I do know that what I saw felt real. An experience that taught me even though Mazen was physically removed from this world, his soul and spirit were becoming strong enough for me to hear a voice and see a person born out of the womb of time and the kingdom of my memories.

As I grieved, the part of me in touch with reality was not aware of an evolutionary process taking place. I wanted to cling to anything that might have given me hope or an opportunity to unite with Mazen in my dreams, or in the external world, something I would have considered a miracle at the time. If I didn't believe in God and the afterlife, I wouldn't know how else to connect with Mazen. I yearned to be with him where we could live together as a family. I ached for an eternal reunion where I could set aside the fear of losing him again and learn to be happy once more. My faith gave me an outlet where dark thoughts became joyful dreams enriched with peace and serenity. I couldn't afford to play "Pascal's Wager," where the philosopher found justification for theism because it was his best bet at the time. God became my friend and if He believes that I'm worthy of His grace, He will reunite me with Mazen. By this, I will leave life alone and accept the notion that I have no control over my destiny or that of my son because if I didn't, my dreams would be black and meaningless. To find peace, I allowed myself to move with the Earth rather than try to steer it.

What brought me comfort in the days and months that followed Mazen's death were the visits, hugs, and close connections with friends and family. I felt the need to hear the soft words and soak in the comforting smiles of those who took time out of their day to show me that they cared. Even my foreign students, who in normal situations were usually shy and reluctant to talk about anything besides homework or classwork, shared their stories of loss and grief. It felt good not only to be heard, but also to listen and find healing in the sometimes horrifying tales of their losses.

With tears streaming down his cheeks, an Iraqi student once told me that one of Saddam's men had forbade his brother from going to medical school. On the day his brother disobeyed the order, not only did they shoot him in the head in front of his parents, but they walked up to his parents and asked them to pay for the bullet. His story was so painful I couldn't help but hold him in my arms and comfort him. My pain still lingered, but at least for the moment, it was shared.

Not all stories were dressed with voices of temporary and magical healing. Some were made of complex syllables that once spoken, would fade into thin air. It hurt to concern myself with the contemplation of people's stories or the contemplation of nature or to even feel that I was part of this world again. The walls of my heart were dressed with black and there was always a deep longing to be with Mazen. In fact, black became my favorite color. It carried a power-draining ambiance that took away the light from my bosom. I had no energy. I felt like I would never be happy again. I thought of traditional Arab women who wore black after the loss of a loved one for decades or until their own death, and I felt like I was one of them. I didn't want to be like them, but like Victor Hugo, I wasn't ready to peel off the dark layers of my guilt and stop wearing black, a color cherished by my blood as a constant reminder of my loss.

A year after Adam awakened in the middle of the night screaming, "There's a ghost in my closet," I swore off my black clothing. I knew that I had to wear colorful clothing again. I consoled myself thinking black wasn't the only thing that fostered my state of connectedness to Mazen; there were reminders of him everywhere. Each time I drove in front of the funeral home where volunteers, friends, and family members had cleansed Mazen of his worldly sins by reciting Quranic verses, my heart would sink. Each time I looked at one of his children or listened to one of his wife's heart-melting stories, I would think of Mazen's face and comforting smile. It was like living in a strange land where stars would weep over the blood-tears that soaked my sheets and the moonlight that engulfed his deathless voice. I imagined him talking to me throughout the day. His voice would pierce my heart as though my memories of him reinforced the universal truth that his physical body had diminished to something intangible. His death was choking me and my thirst for him to be alive was fading like the sun behind the horizon.

I spoke to my internist about my feelings and emotions and after several trials and errors with numerous drugs, I succumbed to Wellbutrin, a non-addictive drug that helped me bridge the gulf between life and death, between then and now, and between acceptance and strength. As much as I was against taking medication when Mazen was ill, I no longer felt the need to control my feelings and emotions. It was no longer about what I could do to fix things; it was about allowing external forces to intervene and remove the bitterness that weighed heavily on my heart. I wanted to read books on grief that promised relief, but I yawned each time I opened a book thinking...*do I really want to read this?* I could not focus on more than a page at a time and the only book that seemed of significant value was *Healing After Loss* by Martha Whitmore Hickman. I could read one page a day and park the odor of mortality in a safe spot until the following day. Battling death was like battling the flame that surrounded the body of Prophet Abraham, the sort of flame that doesn't penetrate the flesh but remains ignited long enough to shake the earth beneath one's feet. Death became the governing master of my beliefs and I felt that no matter what I did, I was going to be haunted by it over the days, months, and years that seemed to have no season. I wrestled in my sleep. I trembled at the thought that there was a possibility I would never see Mazen again—even in the after-life. I was bound in silence. I was locked in a world that swept away my hopes and gave birth to a world that I could only share with those who had a similar experience.

I took Wellbutrin for three years. It helped me walk through my crisis without having to feel crushed by a power beyond my control. It helped me harvest a garden around me that enabled me to see the flowers and breathe the music that gave way to pleasant thoughts and memories of a life long gone, a life that was no more, but a soul that was everlasting. The earth that had once turned black was beginning to turn purple again without me feeling that waking up each morning was a challenge. I no longer tried to unveil the stars or question God's purpose.

When Rabbi Harold S. Kushner wrote about the loss of his daughter in *When Bad Things Happen to Good People,* I realized that God did not take Mazen away from me or take Mazen's life away from him because He wanted to hurt us. God created an imperfect world and it is natural for bad things to happen to any of us. This imperfect world gives room for us to discover how to reach a consensus with time and immortality and how to walk away from the dark clouds and the bitter thoughts of separation to adopt a new life of hope and promise. I'm not sure how this works, but gradually, we learn that we are not alone and that a powerful force is interacting with our senses in ways that will allow us to us to shake off our anger and adopt a new form of wisdom that will lead to peace of mind.

Mazen now dwells in my soul. I see his face and pronounce his name many times throughout the day. There are many things to remind me of him—his children, his widow, and his everlasting passionate smile that flashes in front of me and keeps me in captivity for almost imperceptible, divine moments of peace. His daughter Yasmine and sons Mahmoud and Jemail are the threads connecting me to him. They have inherited many of Mazen's traits and they live in a radiant glow among friends and family members. This leaves me to wonder whether Mazen's soul lingers around them, and the image of his face that decorates every corner of their home dispenses his love and support to them. Robbed of a father from an early age, they walk each year with the rebirth of "spring" to give life to the gardens of their dreams and the hidden treasures of their future. Their mother, who seems to have drawn Mazen into the innermost chamber of her heart, speaks very little of him and the obscure moments of her loss and loneliness.

Mazen's gone and the space that lies between us has established a life of its own. The path is rough, cold, and full of ashes, and I will never be able to collect his remains and turn them into flowers and spices, but I will always have my memories. I have let go of my anger, and adopted a friendship with death. We talk frequently and converse back and forth so that I can communicate with the other side, or simply said, with Mazen. I've accepted Mazen's fate, and I walk through life defining my existence by the joys and sorrows that come my way. I have learned to cherish what I have and to enjoy each living moment with my son Adam, my daughters Rania and Dania, and Mona and my nine grandchildren: Carina, Yasmine, Malik, Mahmoud, Ally, Jemail, Juliana, Rhiana, and baby Mazen, who was named after his deceased uncle.

I know Mazen will never come to me, but I also know I will go to him. I will join him with hope that our reunion will open the gate to a second chance, a chance of welcoming his beaming smile and listening to his chanting voice, when he'll say, "Hi Mom...Are you free? Just want to stop by for coffee. . ."

But when this happens, I won't have to say, "I'm waiting."

Printed in the United States
By Bookmasters